Heidegger and the Poets

Philosophy and Literary Theory

Series Editor: Hugh J. Silverman

Published

Wilhelm S. Wurzer
Filming and Judgment

Véronique M. Fóti
Heidegger and the Poets

Forthcoming

Gianni Vattimo
Consequences of Hermeneutics

Jean-François Lyotard
Toward the Postmodern

Robert Bernasconi
Heidegger in Question

Stephen Barker
Autoaesthetics

* Also available in paperback

Heidegger and the Poets

Poiēsis/Sophia/Technē

—◆—

Véronique M. Fóti

Humanities Press
New Jersey ▼ London

First published 1992 by Humanities Press International, Inc.
Atlantic Highlands, New Jersey 07716, and
3 Henrietta Street, Covent Garden, London WC2E 8LU

© Véronique M. Fóti, 1992

Library of Congress Cataloging-in-Publication Data

Fóti, Véronique Marion.
   Heidegger and the poets : poiēsis/sophia/technē / Véronique M.
Fóti.
      p.   cm.   — (Philosophy and literary theory)
   Includes bibliographical references and index.
   ISBN 0–391–03720–X
   1. Heidegger, Martin, 1889–1976.   2. German poetry—History and
criticism.   I. Title.   II. Series.
   B3279.H49F64   1992
   831.009—dc20   91–9739
                                                                      CIP

A catalogue record for this book is available from the British Library.

Printed in the United States of America

This book is dedicated to my mother and second father,
Jolanda B. Ruppert and Max I. Ruppert,
and to the memory of my father,
Lajos Fóti

What is still possible is a thinking that seeks to grasp the truth of being starting from the monstrous site to which we find ourselves riveted.

Reiner Schürmann, "Riveted to a
Monstrous Site: On Heidegger's
Beiträge zur Philosophie"

Contents

—◆—

CELAN / HEIDEGGER

Prefatory Note

———◆———

Earlier versions of chapters 4 and 6 appeared, under different titles, in *Research in Phenomenology* and in Kathleen Wright, ed., *Festivals of Interpretation*; *Essays on Hans-Georg Gadamer's Work* (Albany: SUNY Press, 1990). Although these essays have been completely reworked to form chapters for the present book, I wish to thank *Research in Phenomenology* and SUNY Press for their gracious permission to recast my earlier writing.

Throughout this book, I have adopted the typographical device of italicizing the *esse* in "essence," to indicate that, for Heidegger, the term *Wesen* is to be understood in such a manner that it bespeaks the Being of beings in its temporal character, rather than the metaphysical concept of essence. Where "essence" is used in its normal sense or in quotation, however, it is given its customary spelling.

Translations from the German and the French (whether poetry or prose) are my own, unless otherwise indicated. References to English translations of the cited texts are in the Notes and Bibliography.

Acknowledgments

◆

Notwithstanding its sustained emphasis on conversation or interlocution (*Gespräch*), the present book has had to be written in virtually complete solitude as well as without institutional support. I wish, however, to express my appreciation to those colleagues and friends who, over the four or five years of the book's gestation, have supported my work, and whose inspiring friendship I have deeply valued. In particular, I wish to thank here Alphonso Lingis, Gene Gendlin, Reiner Schürmann, Edward S. Casey, Wayne Froman, Robert Scharff, David Farrell Krell, Mary C. Rawlinson, James R. Watson, and Marcella Tarrozzi-Goldsmith.

The book owes, indeed, a special debt to a searching conversation that Gene Gendlin initiated and pursued with me at the 1989 SPEP (Society for Phenomenology and Existential Philosophy) meeting in Pittsburgh, a conversation concerning the larger focus of my work on Heidegger and the poets. I think that Gene will recognize the fruit of that conversation throughout the book.

Special thanks are due to some wonderful graduate and undergraduate students who have worked with me over the years, especially to Silvia Benso, whose own work on Heidegger has been inspiring to me, and to Jack Wood, who, as my graduate assistant in 1990, went out of his way to give me more time for my work and who painstakingly and insightfully proofread several chapters.

Vera Mark of the French Department at the Pennsylvania State University, her husband R. Nagarajan, and Monique Yaari, likewise of the French Department, have been invaluable friends. Vera and Nagu, with the help of visiting aunts, enabled me to keep body and soul together with a weekly South Indian meal during the summer of 1990, when the intensity of my writing took precedence over bodily needs.

I would also like to express my gratitude to the Fulbright Foundation for granting me a lectureship in India for the fall of 1987. In Varanasi, Professor Annakutty V. K. Findeis, of the German Department at Benares Hindu

University, kindly extended me her generous hospitality, and we then discovered our shared engagement with the poetry of Paul Celan. I profited much from discussions with Annakutty and, while I do not know her present whereabouts, I hope that this book will reach her hands. May it also constitute a gesture of appreciation to the many Indian scholars and colleagues—from the Indian Institute of Advanced Research in Simla (then directed by Dr. Margaret Chatterjee) to North Bengal University, and to the universities of Madras and Mysore—who received me with a warmth and interest far beyond simple collegiality.

Special thanks are due to the series editor, Professor Hugh Silverman, for his interest in and encouragement of my work, his conscientious reading of the manuscript, and his helpful suggestions. I also wish to thank the president of Humanities Press, Keith Ashfield, and the production editor, Ms. Katherine Steinberger, as well as other staff members involved in seeing my book through the stages of production, for their professional expertise and helpfulness.

My deepest thanks, however, go to my children, Sunil G. Sharma, Leila Sharma, Ravi K. Sharma, and Amina Sharma, who have borne with me much of the itinerant existence and hardship of my years in academe, and whose fortitude, creativity, love and friendship continues, above all, to sustain me. To my son Ravi I also owe a professional debt for his undertaking the computer production of my notes and bibliography with exemplary competence and scrupulous care.

Abbreviations

$\blacklozenge$

Complete bibliographical references are in the Bibliography and Notes.

BW   David Farrell Krell, ed., *Heidegger: Basic Writings*

FA   Hölderlin, *Sämtliche Werke. Frankfurter historisch-kritische Ausgabe*

GA   Heidegger, *Gesamtausgabe*

HAP   Philippe Lacoue-Labarthe, *Heidegger, Art and Politics*

PC   Paul Celan, *Gesammelte Werke*

PLT   Albert Hofstadter, ed., *Heidegger: Poetry, Language, Thought*

SA   Hölderlin, *Sämtliche Werke. Grosse Stuttgarter Ausgabe*

Introduction

◆

Doch ist es heilsamer für das Denken, wenn
es im Befremdlichen wandert, statt sich im
Verständlichen einzurichten.

Martin Heidegger,

*But it is more salutary for thinking to wander
in estrangement than to establish itself in the
comprehensible.*

This book maps out the parameters and configurations of a terrain of the
estrangement of both poetry and "thinking" (as distinct from "philosophy"), opened up by what Heidegger calls the "destinal interlocution"
(*Gespräch*) between poet and thinker. Although both poetry and thinking
are startlingly divested of their traditional identities in being drawn into this
terrain, Heidegger considers that, in their estrangement, they are also at last
restored to what is most deeply their own: to the unconstrained *apophansis*
of language that enables all manifestation and that repudiates any metaphysical ground.

It will be helpful to clarify at the outset that the German terms *das
Dichten* and *die Dichtung* are not precisely synonymous with the English
term "poetry" but are, in fact, closer to the Greek (and hence also Platonic)
notion of *poiēsis*. Although both these terms generally mean "poetry" in the
usual sense, they also serve to denote literary creation *simpliciter*. Thus, Paul
Celan can speak of Georg Büchner's *Dichtung*, which comprises drama and
narrative; and Heidegger himself speaks of Greek tragedy as the highest
Dichtung (see chapters 5 and 6, below).

Heidegger's own animadversions about "literature," and his frequent
insistence that his own lectures and texts on poetry need to be dissociated

from literary scholarship (*Literaturwissenschaft*) and from the whole "business of literature" (*Literaturbetrieb*), must therefore *not* be read as an attempt to dissever poetry from literature and to accord it a mysterious if not mystical privilege. It would, to say the least, be odd if Heidegger were to bring together thinking and poetizing through their *essential* relationship to language, while excluding "literature" (which he so often refers to in his elucidations of passages of poetry) from this bond. What he criticizes under the rubric of *Literaturbetrieb*, is an academic and culturally sanctioned mode of the production of discourse about literary works, which, in his judgment, obscures the crucial aspects of *Dichtung*: its relationship, through language, to the enigma of manifestation (indicated by the rather shopworn term "Being") and its role in configuring the historical (and political) economies of presencing—in other words, precisely those aspects that bring it into interlocution with a thinking freed, as much as possible, of its own metaphysical (and institutional) cathexes.

If one keeps this broader meaning of *Dichtung* in mind, and if one is also willing to deliteralize and rethink Merleau-Ponty's notion of "perception" (as it figures in his late work), so that it becomes the differential "trait" of manifestation, one can recognize the kinship between Heidegger's engagement with *Dichtung* and Merleau-Ponty's insistence that "Being requires creation of us," and that there can hence be neither pure intuition nor pure production.[1]

Heidegger articulates this insight through the problematic of *technē*, with its double kinship to *poiēsis*, on the one hand, and to metaphysical reason, modern science, and contemporary technicity, on the other. Despite their *essential* bond, Greek *technē* and contemporary technicity are, for Heidegger, in polar tension, in that the former (as technical or craft production or as art) is an inherently *differential* modality of un-concealment, whereas the latter reveals beings (including human beings) in the manner of reductive totalization. Technicity, therefore, tends toward the nadir of oblivion of the differential character of manifestation, which, in Greek thought, harmoniously conjoins *technē* with the spontaneous presencing of *physis*. In a 1967 lecture delivered in Athens, Heidegger delineates the self-referential closure of reductive totalization as "the circle of the rule" (*Regelkreis*), and comments as follows:

> The cybernetic projection of the world, the "victory of method over science," enables a thoroughly uniform and, in this sense, universal calculability, *i.e.*, the governability of the lifeless world as well as the world of life. Human beings also are drawn into this uniformity of the cybernetic world—they, indeed, in a privileged way [by taking on the role of subject] . . . Cybernetically represented, the subject-object relationship is the correlation of information, the re-coupling within the privileged

circle of the rule, which can be circumscribed by the title of "man and world."[2]

Both "cybernetic" and political totalization are, for Heidegger, the *essential* consequences of technicity. They are, therefore, assimilated to the point of being indiscriminable; to the extent that Heidegger voices criticisms of political ideologies (as he does frequently but unsystematically in the lecture courses of 1934–1944/45), his comments are not concretely political but remain focused on the differential character of manifestation and the disclosive power of language that totalization occludes.

Several strands of Heidegger's thinking are interlinked at this juncture. First of all, he holds that, even though the reductive totalization of technicity constitutes the extremity of the "danger" involved in all un-concealment, technicity or "posture" (*Ge-stell*) still remains a modality of the granting of manifestation. As such, it harbors within itself the possibility of another and more salutary understanding, which, Heidegger insists, is not a theoretical prelude to *praxis* but is itself action and is historically transformative. This other understanding cannot be brought about through human ingenuity but presupposes a reflective questioning of the "posture," which requires, in its turn, that there should be an initial breach or rupture in "the circle of the rule." Given the original bond that, for Heidegger, links technicity to Greek *technē* and thus to *poiēsis*, he finds this breach, which promises a "saving" from danger, in the genuine work of art that accomplishes a compelling presencing withdrawn from calculability and reductive explanation. While Heidegger agrees with Hegel concerning the fundamentally aletheic character of art and art-works, he disagrees with him concerning their onto-historical situation; for he considers the fullness of the disclosive power of art still waiting to be realized over against the tightening of the closure of *essential* technicity. The following passage from the Athens lecture elucidates this disclosive power:

> Must not the work as work point into what is not at man's disposal, what conceals itself, so that the work may say more than just what one already knows, recognizes, and busies oneself about? Must not the work of art bestow silence upon that which conceals itself [and] which, in its self-concealment, awakens in human beings respect (*Scheu*) before what cannot be planned or governed, calculated or fabricated?[3]

To pick up another strand of Heidegger's thinking: art is not only *essentially* "poetic," in that it is *poiēsis* free of the constraints of *arkhē*-telic economies of presencing, but also in that, due to the primordially apophantic character of language, poetry or *Dichtung* has, for Heidegger, priority among the arts.[4] The poets then, are those who first of all breach the circle of the rule and leave it marked with the traces of rupture.

Precisely in that these traces involve a certain bestowal of silence, however, they do not cry out for attention; they may be hermetic or, as Heidegger prefers to put it, dislocated into the *essential unsaid*. Heidegger believes, therefore, that they must be decrypted, that such decrypting is the task of the thinker's "elucidations," and that the thinker's mediation must render the ruptures decisive, so as to prepare for a new historical beginning.

Given Heidegger's sense (which is perhaps most acute in the 1930s and 1940s, but which seems never to have left him) of living through a momentous historical crisis, which is the crisis of modernity, he considers it imperative for historically responsible thinking to achieve an insight into planetary technicity as the aletheic configuration of modernity. In quest of such insight (which would allow thinking to seize the historical moment), he finds it necessary to problematize anew the Western philosophical tradition and to return to the very origins of Western thought, while recognizing that *the manner of thinking* which governs this tradition has exhausted itself and needs to be both deconstructed and supplanted.

To think the tradition otherwise than it has articulated itself, to think it forward into an as yet nameless transition requires, Heidegger holds, that thinking should heed the pathbreaking "saying" of destinal poets. The poet whose *essential* unsaid awaits, above all, the thinker's retrieval, for the sake of the future of Germany and of the entire West, is, on his understanding, Hölderlin—the more so since Hölderlin is himself engaged in a transforming retrieval of ancient Greece. As concerns Heidegger's conception of the destinal role of the German *Volk* as a "metaphysical people," and as a people situated in the very heart of Europe, the following passage, dating from 1935, is revealing and characteristic:

> But out of this determination, of which we are assured, this people will only make a destiny for itself if it first creates *in itself* an echo, the possibility of an echo of this determination . . . All this involves that this people, as historical, should place itself, and therewith the history of the Occident, out of the midst of its future happening into the originary domain of the powers of Being. Precisely if the great decision about Europe is not to eventuate on the path of annihilation, it can eventuate only through the unfolding of new spiritual powers from out of the middle.[5]

The *hybris* of Heidegger's assumption of the role of destinal thinker, who is to transpose the withheld promise of the Western intellectual tradition into the awaited future, and who is to restore its poets and thinkers to what is most truly their own, scarcely needs to be pointed out. As concerns Hölderlin, Heidegger disregards the tenuous (and changing) character of his intellectual constructs and literalizes the poet's task of preparing a historical site for destinal transformation. The other poets whom Heidegger situates in

Hölderlin's *Wirkungsgeschichte*, notably Trakl and Rilke, are conformed to the procrustean bed of this *ess*ential-historical reading, often in disregard of *lexis* and of the autofiguration of their poetry.

Heidegger's interlocution with the poets thus does not constitute a "poetic" retreat from "real philosophy," nor yet from the historical and political scene. It remains intimately connected both to his transformative reading of Greek and modern thought and to his crypto-politics. Its uncanny conflation of penetrating philosophical analysis with historical interpretation, with spiritual and ideological motifs, and with aesthetic subtleties needs to be problematized rather than espoused, ignored, or dismissed. This book traces its own genesis to what was at first an inchoate but persistently troubling awareness of a deflection in Heidegger's readings of his chosen poets, which occludes transgression, excess, or loss and constrains the poetry to fit the exigencies of an *ess*ential if always "polemic" (or differential) unification. A problematizing of Heidegger's unifying moves gradually brought into view the structures and dynamics of the complex conflations indicated.

Heidegger's deflections and conflations have the fundamental character of an aesthetization of the political (conjoined with a mythical recasting of history); as Lacoue-Labarthe has insisted, such aesthetization constitutes the key aspect of his involvement with National Socialism.[6] The present book is mindful of this issue throughout but addresses it most explicitly in problematizing Heidegger's refusal to extend his interlocution to Paul Celan (while Celan sought out such interlocution by his own initiative). What makes this refusal important is not only that Celan writes out of the experience of the Holocaust but also that he both situates his poetry in relation to Hölderlin and criticizes and repudiates the aesthetization of the political, whereas Heidegger develops his own aesthetization in dialogue with Hölderlin.

The landscape of the terrain of estrangement, which dislocates poetry into *ess*ential thinking, and philosophy into an interlocution with poetry, is stranger perhaps than its captivating initial appearance might lead one to suspect. No exhaustive or systematic mapping of this terrain has been undertaken in the present book, which offers, instead, a series of in-depth regional explorations. For this approach there are several reasons.

First of all, the philosophical and poetic texts under consideration require a concentrated intensity of reading, rather than a thematic appropriation. This is equally true of the Heideggerian texts (which, after years of reading, continue to reveal new aspects and unsuspected complexities), and of the verse and prose writings of the poets, particularly Hölderlin and Celan. A close and laborious reading of the poetic texts is also mandated by the fact that the present book reproaches Heidegger, quite generally, with a disregard of *lexis*. The aim of such a reading is not an exegetical repetition of the texts, nor yet their scholarly representation, but a participation in their labor of articulation, in the very dynamics of their self-configuration. Such participation cannot, of course, relinquish its critical vigilance, especially as concerns Heidegger's crypto-politics.

The texts, furthermore, are not read in isolation but in their intercrossings and ambiguous interpenetrations, and hence in a way that is mindful of an ongoing displacement of proper closure. Moreover, they often problematize their own articulation as well as the powers of language, so that any totalizing interpretation would betray them. Even Heidegger's notion of the *essential* unsaid emerges, in this perspective, as a totalizing move. Rather than being represented or systematized, the texts must be read at once in their finitude and in their transgression of closure.

The order of the present book is not chronological, with respect either to the development of Heidegger's thought or to the historical relationships among the poets discussed. Heidegger's interlocution with Hölderlin, for instance, receives a weighty position near the book's center, and in fitting proximity to the chapters concerned with Celan, rather than near the beginning in keeping with the chronology of *Wirkungsgeschichte*. The book's order, however, is not merely a matter of suitable arrangement, but reflects, in its very "regionalism," the development of a guiding thought.

This thought or concern takes its bearings from Levinas's critique that Heidegger's thought of Being, "in subordinating every relation with the existent to the relation with Being . . . affirms the primacy of freedom over ethics." Freedom is not understood here as free will but as "the mode of remaining the same in the midst of the other"; it is contrasted with justice, which binds one to the Other (the personal Other), namely, to "an existent that refuses to give itself," with the bond of an irrecusable obligation.[7]

One must certainly agree that the ethical import of Heidegger's questioning of the alterity and irreducible difference involved in the structure of manifestation remains undeveloped in his thinking, and even that certain themes of this thinking (notably its preoccupation with historical instauration) impede and frustrate such development. To the extent that an ontological ethics that is an ethics of alterity announces itself in an inchoate way in Heidegger's meditations, it takes the form of a poetically instituted human dwelling upon the earth, which respects and responds to the enigma of manifestation. The questions of how such a respect for ontological alterity can announce and concretize itself in one's relationships with the human and non-human Other (which latter is neglected by Levinas), how it can inform and transform the structures of community, how it is to be situated with respect to the Western ethical tradition, and finally, how it is to identify and challenge evil, all remain largely or entirely neglected. To address these questions will be a crucial task of the thinking that today follows (but does not merely explicate or repeat) Heidegger. This book problematizes Heidegger's aesthetization and obscuration of the ethical in his interlocution with the poets, in preparation for the more "constructive" task indicated.

A questioning that is oriented toward a concretized ethics of alterity, indeed (in sharp contrast to Heidegger's orientation), toward an "ethization" of aesthetic concerns, is characteristic of the poet from whom Heidegger withheld his interlocution, Paul Celan. Significantly, however, Celan, in struggling against menacing despair for a poetic articulation (informed by both Hölderlin and Mallarmé) that responds to the Other's extremity, continues (to a greater extent than has so far been realized) to engage with and problematize Heideggerian thought-structures. An important strand of this engagement is traced below in chapter 7.

As Reiner Schürmann has observed, one is hard pressed to find in contemporary philosophy "a thought that raises even so much as the question of the conditions of what has happened to us" in this century, in the time of both Heidegger's and Celan's writing. Heidegger, whatever his blind spots, in striving painfully to extricate himself (no doubt incompletely) from his ideological entanglements, has at least clearly perceived the need "to think otherwise the one question supposed *originarily* to remain open . . . the question of Being."[8] If other questions—such as the question of evil—cannot be closed, Schürmann adds, it is precisely because they issue from the question of manifestation, with an issuance which, of course, is not foundational.

If Heidegger did not adequately address the development of an ethics of alterity from a questioning of the differential character of manifestation— indeed, if he impeded its development—he at least renders possible an in-depth problematizing of this obstructed issuance. The interlocution between poetry and thinking which he instigates is a groping in this direction, a detour perhaps, but one made necessary in good part by the failure of philosophy proper to speak to the issues. The very task of such an interlocution (as explained in chapter 7) is to bring into interrelation the severity of a philosophically informed questioning of the stucture of manifestation, and an articulation of the ethical/aesthetic relationship to the Other in its alterity and in the compelling singularity of its presencing.

1

◆

Phainesthai, Beauty, Semblance: Reading Mörike

Der Dichtungscharakter des Denkens ist noch
verhüllt. Wo er sich zeigt, gleicht er für lange
Zeit der Utopie eines halbpoetischen Verstandes.

M. Heidegger, "Aus der Erfahrung des Denkens"

The poetic character of thinking still remains veiled.
Where it does show itself, it resembles for a long
time the utopia of a half-poetical understanding.

In a lecture on "The Art of Interpretation" offered in Amsterdam and Freiburg in 1950,[1] Emil Staiger advised the practitioners of German *Literaturwissenschaft* (the discipline or science of literary scholarship) to subordinate scientific methodology to the primacy of an intuitive engagement with the "spirit" animating a particular work, a spirit discernible as "rhythm," which forms the basis of style. Prominent among the schools of interpretation he criticizes is that of literary and intellectual history (*Geistesgeschichte*), which tends to "surrender the literary work of art to the philosophers" and then perceives in it only "what any thinker understands much better than any poet does."[2]

As concerns lyric poetry, such interpreters are partial to difficult poems, "full of abstract thought," but have little to contribute to the reading of an unpretentious poem that is both intelligible and short, yet poses the challenge of an engagement with "the genuinely poetic." Staiger chooses, for his own exemplary interpretation, a simple poem, classical in inspiration and form and written by a poet who (despite his reading of Hölderlin's *Hyperion*, as well

1

as some personal access to the late Hölderlin)³ remains apart from Hölderlin's *Wirkungsgeschichte* or historical efficacy. The poem is Eduard Mörike's "Auf eine Lampe," written in 1846:

> Noch unverrückt, o schöne Lampe, schmückest du,
> An leichten Ketten zierlich aufgehangen hier,
> Die Decke des nun fast vergessnen Lustgemachs.
> Auf deiner weissen Marmorschale, deren Rand
> Der Efeukranz von goldengrünem Erz umflicht,
> Schlingt fröhlich eine Kinderschar den Ringelreihn.
> Wie reizend alles! lachend, und ein sanfter Geist
> Des Ernsten doch umgossen um die ganze Form—
> Ein Kunstgebild der echten Art. Wer achtet sein?
> Was aber schön ist, selig scheint es in ihm selbst.⁴

Staiger's reading of the poem emphasizes the sense of disseverance and gentle melancholy characteristic of Mörike's poetic voice, particularly in his later poems (which include "Auf eine Lampe"). In these poems, Staiger observes, Mörike's earlier fascination with time and with the continuity of memory has yielded place to clear spatial definition, in the context of which the poet marks and remarks "an unfulfilled space." In keeping with Mörike's historical situation as an epigone of the brilliant Goethe period, the "social and cosmopolitan goals" of that period are occluded; and beauty, in particular, is no longer accorded a transformative educational role but presents itself as "a respite, a remnant, an unfulfilled space" in an alien environment. The future, as Staiger observes, is "missing in Mörike's poetry."⁵

In this poem, Staiger finds "the purest omitted space" to be the one marked by the baroque term *Lustgemach* (festive room), a term already obsolescent if not obsolete in Mörike's time. This room, for which language has lost the word, is the one in which the beautiful lamp still hangs undisplaced. A second prominent mark of disseverance for Staiger is the verb *scheint*, in the last verse, which he reads as "seems." Thus read, it indicates the poet's inability or unwillingness to voice a straightforward and confident Goethean statement about beauty's intrinsic nature. Indeed, Mörike's recourse to the Swabian dialect form "in ihm selbst," instead of the High German "in sich selbst," contributes a consummate refinement: it serves, by its very indirection, to place the beautiful at an infrangible remove from human possession and valuation.

Staiger concludes the lecture with an un-Heideggerian tribute to humanistic vision, which "perhaps points to a goal not yet accessible" while, at the same time, opening up "the unfathomable depth of art."⁶

Heidegger, in the first of two letters to Staiger (GA 13, 95–97),[7] advocates the hermeneutical approach of reading Mörike's poem "backwards," by allowing the last two verses to open up the sense of the whole. These two verses, he points out, "express *in nuce* Hegel's aesthetics," in that the lamp, as "an art-formation of the genuine sort," functions here as a *symbolon*[8] of the art-work as such (which is, for Hegel, the Ideal). As a beautiful artistic creation that is also, in its form, a lamp, this particular work consummately unites sensuous radiance (*scheinen*) and the manifestness of the Idea (as *Erscheinung*), which constitutes, for Hegel, the essence of the work of art. Moreover, the poem, as itself an artistic creation which rests within the privileged domain of language, can be considered a *symbolon* of the art-work as such.[9]

The hermeneutical approach proposed by Heidegger provides a firm basis for the interpretation of Mörike's *scheint* (instead of just motivating the "doubts" and "misgivings" which Staiger attributes to certain other scholars): in Latin paraphrase, Heidegger insists, the phrase "selig scheint es in ihm selbst" is to be read as "feliciter lucet in eo ipso" (shines blessedly in itself) rather than as "felix in se ipso esse videtur" (seems to be blessed within itself). The very Being of the beautiful is *phainesthai* in its pure radiance.

For Hegel, Heidegger points out, *phainesthai* means the sensuous radiance of the Idea, which is, in itself, the "higher truth" of the sensuous manifestations (*Erscheinungen*) presented by art.[10] In availing himself of the same Swabian idiom ("an ihm selbst") as Mörike,[11] Hegel gives it a precise meaning: it indicates that which, in its manifestations, is not "in itself (*in sich*) free and self-conscious."[12] Heidegger emphasizes that, for Hegel, the structure of the phenomenal self-manifestation of the Idea is not one of adequation or *mimēsis* but rather of revelatory presencing as *apophansis* or *parousia*. Hegel can thus consider self-sufficient serenity or blessedness to be the fundamental trait of the Ideal and, together with it, of the work of art.

Such considerations, of course, do not serve to establish that Mörike gave any heed to these Hegelian thought-structures—the more so since, as Staiger, in his response (GA 13, 97–100),[13] is quick to point out, he lacked both interest in and aptitude for theoretical thought. It is, however, emphatically not Heidegger's concern to delineate causal relationships but rather (as regards the references to Hegel) to indicate a certain intellectual context or "atmosphere" in which Mörike's work is situated:

> I maintain that one who is a poet need not concern himself with philosophy, but that a poet becomes all the more one who poetizes, the more he becomes one who thinks. (From Heidegger's second letter, GA 13, 100–108)[14]

Staiger's response, by contrast, marshals the scholarly resources of the literary historian in the interest of establishing that Mörike's poetic genius is remote from the precise determinations of theory, and that, indeed, the "old fox" (he emphasizes the poet's cunning) enjoyed ambiguity (such as that between *lucet* and *videtur* in *scheint*) for the sake of the resonance and iridescence of his poetic language. However, Staiger determines, the tentativeness of *scheinen* as semblance epitomizes Mörike's existential situation; and Heidegger's "scholasticism" is in danger of obscuring "the precious individual color" of this poet's art.

Heidegger's thoughtful and closely argued reply points out, first of all, that the issue, for him, is "something other" than the correct interpretation of an isolated verse; this "other," he adds cryptically, "will decide, perhaps soon, perhaps in a distant time, but certainly first, and even alone, the relationship of language to us mortals" (GA 13, 100).[15]

With implied reference to his discussion of phenomenon and *logos*, in section seven of *Being and Time*,[16] Heidegger points out that the *scheinen* of semblance, in its various forms, is founded upon pure *phainesthai*, in the sense of phenomenal presencing. The Greek sense of *phainetai*, he notes, differs from that of the Latin *videtur*, even where mere semblance is denoted, for the Latin term is thought from the point of view of the observer, rather than from out of the unconstrained spontaneity of presencing. In Hegel's use of the terminology of *scheinen* in the context of a philosophy of art, the sense and architectonic of the Greek concept of the phenomenal, Heidegger indicates, is preserved and developed (hence the importance of Hegel here for Heidegger's own rethinking of the phenomenological phenomenon). As concerns Mörike, he notes that the Hegelian thought-structures in question inform the intellectual horizons of 19th-century Germany and, indeed, the very spirit of the language (*Sprachgeist*), without, for all that, being grasped explicitly or with a high level of understanding. The poet's philosophical disinclination does not argue against a quasi-Hegelian reading.

Heidegger agrees with Staiger concerning the need to become attuned to a poem's fundamental mood (*Grundstimmung*); he also concurs in identifying the mood of Mörike's poem as one of melancholy or even nostalgia. He further accepts (although without "effacements") Staiger's structural articulation of the poem according to a schema of $3 \times 3 + 1$, or perhaps $3 \times 2 + 2 \times 2$ (the Dantesque allusion of the former schema is noted by Staiger; the Pythagorean symbolism of the number ten may also be significant). Within these fairly conventional constraints, Heidegger offers an extraordinary reading.

The first three verses, he finds, show the lamp's mode of presencing (as an art-work) to be a "lighting" and "adorning," which allow a certain aspect of a vanished lifeworld to stand revealed. What is thus shown forth is gathered into its *essencing* (denoted by the Hegelian term *gewesen*).

In the following three verses, the lamp's visible aspect is presented as that in and through which the *essential* revealing is accomplished. Mörike characterizes "the entire form" of the lamp as pervaded at once by charm or laughter and by seriousness. Heidegger reads this conjunction as the counterplay between "ravishment" (*Berückung*) and "transport" (*Entrückung*), in terms of which he defines the character (*Wesen*) of the beautiful in his 1940 lecture on Hölderlin's hymn "Wie wenn am Feiertage . . ." (GA 4, 49–77). The "transport" is a differential uniting, whereas the "ravishment" is the extreme self-assertion of a phenomenal singularity. While this intimate "contrariety" or strife that defines the beautiful recalls the strife between Earth and World in Heidegger's analysis of the revelatory character of the work of art,[17] it does not have the same epochal-historical focus but is more Anaximandrian, as well as topological, in inspiration. The cited Hölderlin essay also illumines Heidegger's understanding of *Schein* in its relation to the beautiful. Concerning Hölderlin's "divinely beautiful nature" as the very element of the poet, Heidegger writes:

> And nature is called "divinely beautiful" because a god or a goddess are most likely to awaken, in their appearing (*Erscheinen*), the semblance (*Schein*) of ravishment and transport. But in truth they are not capable of the beautiful in its purity, for their particular appearing (*Erscheinen*) remains semblance (*Schein*), because mere ravishment ("epiphany") looks like transport, and mere transport (into mystical absorption) gives itself as ravishment. Nevertheless, the god is capable of the highest semblance (*Schein*) of the beautiful and thus approaches most closely to the pure appearing (*Erscheinen*) of all-presence.
> (GA 4, 54)

Leaving aside the question of the Hegelian relationship between art, religion, and spirit, it is remarkable that Heidegger considers the beautiful, *phainesthai*, in its purity, to be inaccessible as such, requiring the detour of semblance, and that he accords to the figure of the (awaited) divinity the highest semblance of the beautiful.

Noting that the art-work's "entire form," or *Gestalt*, pervaded by the counterplay of ravishment and transport, is presented in verses seven and eight as "that which presences set into the appearing of its full visibility," Heidegger turns to the problematic concluding verses. If the beauty of the lamp has already been brought into its full radiance—why does the poem continue? What has not yet come to word, Heidegger finds, is the "genuine kind" of this art-work or thing of beauty—beauty as such.

Although the thing of beauty may be withdrawn from an age in which few give it heed, the very Being of the beautiful remains, Heidegger insists, independent of human valuation or its lack. Its independence does not betray ahistoricity (as with the Platonic *eidos* of Beauty) but rather the sheer enigma of *phainesthai*, which involves and claims man rather than being within the domain of human mastery. This enigma, however, can only be glimpsed from out of history, through the presencing of a "world" in its *essential* configuration; and such presencing, in turn, requires the compelling radiance (*scheinen*) of the beautiful:

> The beautiful can accomplish this only insofar as it illumines through its intrinsic (*in ihm*) radiance, *i.e.*, in shining. Because this is what "shining" means, and because the "in itself" (*in ihm*) belongs with it, the poem, in its last words, returns to the initial ones": Still undisplaced, oh beautiful lamp . . ."
> (GA 13, 106)[18]

Having thus closed the serene figure of Mörike's circle (the circle-shape of the lamp as well as of the poem), Heidegger comments on the consummate refinement of presenting the art-work in the form of a lamp, which, given that lighting and irradiating are proper to it, exemplifies or symbolizes the revelatory character of the art-work or thing of beauty. He is careful to note that this refinement does not require that the lamp be actually lit.

No mood of melancholy touches, in the end, the beautiful in its serene withdrawal from those who pass it by unheeded. Nevertheless, Heidegger surmises, the epigone may see farther than the initiated and thus suffer more from the degradation of *phainesthai* to mere appearance.

Staiger's brief and appreciative reply (GA 13, 108f)[19] contents itself with correcting a possible misunderstanding: Mörike's *scheint* is not, on his interpretation, the "seeming" of semblance but rather of hesitancy and tentativeness. He emphasizes, once again, his commitment to reading the poet in his individuality rather than in terms of philosophical thought-structures.

Staiger's publication of the exchange between Heidegger and himself provoked a critical essay by Leo Spitzer, to which Staiger appended a brief response.[20] Spitzer completely disregards Heidegger's admonition that what is at stake is "other" than a question of textual interpretation, and his essay is as philosophically unperceptive as it is erudite and astute in its philological and literary critique. His sarcastic caricature of Heidegger's rhetorical style earns him Staiger's reproof.

Spitzer points out that "Auf eine Lampe" belongs to the tradition of the thing-poem (*Dinggedicht*)—a tradition which allows the poet to efface his or her individuality and intellectual preoccupations in favor of showing forth a natural entity or artefact.[21] Mörike's poem does not, he asserts, offer any theory of beauty but presents, instead, "a lyric experience of beauty." Furthermore, Spitzer also considers it a figure-poem in that its own articulation and poetic form instantiate the form of the lamp and give concretion to the serenity symbolized by the circle that returns into itself. Spitzer does not address the difference between an artistic or poetic presentation of the thing-Being of *things* (for example, Van Gogh's painting of shoes, which Heidegger discusses in "The Origin of the Work of Art") and a similar presentation of the *art-work* or thing of beauty. He contents himself, instead, with emphasizing the poem's "organic integration" of artistic and philosophical vision with sensuous perception.

Although Spitzer declares himself to be more inclined toward Heidegger's reading of *scheint* than Staiger's, he insists that the issue of luminosity, or radiance versus semblance, is irrelevant, since the lamp remains unlit and is considered entirely from the point of view of its plastic form. Heidegger, of course, does not dispute this, and his comment that "the poem does not light the lamp; but it lights up the beautiful lamp" (GA 13, 104),[22] far from being what Spitzer calls "a precious pomp of words," makes a precise point: it is the poem which allows the "lighting and adorning" mode of presencing proper to the thing of beauty to come into its own. Hence, even where such a thing is neglected and disregarded, where the beautiful lamp remains unlit, the poem, so to speak, restores its *essen*tial function in superabundance. Spitzer's animadversions about luminosity also fail to do justice to the prevalence of fire and light imagery in Mörike's poems. One can cite here, almost at random, the "reflected glow" (*Widerschein*), the flickering, burning, and kindling of "Peregrina," the fiery radiance (*Schein*) and leaping sparks of "Das verlassene Mägdlein," or the brilliance of lightning (*Wetterschein*) in "Erinna an Sappho." Even Mörike's "Auf eine Buche," which Spitzer cites as a parallel thing-poem that also celebrates the serenely balanced and protective form of the circle, contains the following verses:

> Wo den beschatteten Kreis die feurig strahlende Sonne,
> Fast gleich messend umher säumte mit blendendem
> Rand . . .[23]

It is, of course, this precise feature of Mörike's poetry which renders this very un-Hölderlinian poet, the "son" not of Pindar but "of Horace," important to Heidegger.

Spitzer, in conclusion, devotes his philological skills to an analysis of *scheinen*, which, in the Swabian dialect that both Staiger and Heidegger emphasize, carries the meaning of "to be beautiful" or "to be resplendent." Spitzer concludes that Mörike's last verse is to be read as the almost tautological statement that what is beautiful is inherently resplendent. He seeks, quite incomprehensibly, to dissociate luminosity from splendor, and does not see that the assimilation of phenomenal radiance to the splendor of beauty in the Swabian dialect brings home Heidegger's guiding concern.

Similarly, he offers an insightful commentary on the unconstrained spontaneity and informality of Mörike's diction in the verse "Was aber schön ist . . .," while completely neglecting Heidegger's concern with the unconstrained spontaneity of manifestation as *phainesthai.*

It is time, then, to ask what is the "something other" which is the focus of Heidegger's concern, and which Spitzer bypasses; whereas Staiger dimly perceives it to be "language," although he is unable to bring it into meaningful relation with the issue of *phainesthai.*

To consider this question, it will be helpful to turn to another Heideggerian text, which is nearly contemporaneous with the letters on Mörike and which casts the issues into sharper focus—the 1951 essay "Logos," which addresses certain Heraclitean fragments.[24] This text is also valuable for its concern with the initial Greek articulation of the problematic. Whereas Spitzer is quick to assimilate Heidegger's thought of *phainesthai* to "the whole of light metaphysics" (implicitly reading Heidegger's references to Hegel as a reaffirmation of Hegelianism), Heidegger, in fact, seeks to exceed the Hegelian completion of metaphysics by a renewed problematizing of early Greek thought. Finally, since a rethinking of *logos* and *legein* (as *die Lese* and *lesen*) is closely linked to the question of what it means to read, the essay is instructive regarding Heidegger's final comment in his second letter to Staiger: not the poem, but "we" stand in need of the thinking he has just undertaken, so as simply to learn, not primarily to read poems, but to read.

In its originary sense, Heidegger indicates, *legein*, like the German *lesen*, means a gathering together that selects and elects, with a view to laying out and laying up (*hinterlegen, bergen, keisthai*) what is thus gathered, to letting it announce itself as *hypokeimenon*. In this laying out, however, *legein* is not concerned to bring that which lies before into its lay, that is, to constrain it in conformity with any project (such as the mathematical-metaphysical project of modernity). It is concerned, rather, to safeguard, in its lucid articulation, the unconstrained spontaneity of presencing and the differential character of manifestation. The crucial point, then, for the present analysis, is that *logos*, as this gathering and gathered letting-lie-before (as language and saying), does not create or impose the configurations of presencing but rather responds to the (epochal) spontaneity of unconcealment. *Logos* is properly the a-venue of manifestation, the accomplishment of *phainesthai*:

> For saying receives its *essential* determination out of the unconcealedness of what together lies before. But the revealment (*Entbergung*) of the concealed into the unconcealed is itself the presencing (*Anwesen*) of what presences (*des Anwesenden*). We call it the Being of beings.[25]

Logos, or *legein*, is thus emphatically not a human doing; it carries neither authority nor the trappings of authorship[26] and is not analyzable in terms of expression or meaning (*Ausdruck* and *Bedeutung*). *Legein* is rather *apophainesthai*, the accomplishment of what, with reference to Mörike, was called a "shining" in and of itself. Such *apophainesthai* is no longer the phenomenological phenomenon (which latter lacks an essential relationship to *logos*), for the reason that it restores what it brings into presencing to its essential concealment, which is to say, to the Differing. With respect to Heraclitus, Heidegger articulates the latter as *hen/panta*. This "restoring" of the phenomenon to concealment happens, so to speak, in the very "act" of bringing it into presencing (*Anwesen*, which must be carefully distinguished from sheer presence or *Anwesenheit*).[27]

The remaining question, then, is *how* a phenomenal unconcealment which safeguards the enigma of presencing can be accomplished, and what, in particular, is the role here of poetic *logos*, and of beauty as the traditional prerogative of poetry and art in general.

In the 1953/54 text "Aus einem Gespräch von der Sprache" (GA 12, 81–146),[28] which recreates an interlocution with Professor Tezuka of Tokyo Imperial University, Heidegger warns that the philosophical language of interlocution threatens to occlude and even destroy what is at issue. This danger, which arises from the tacit, unnoticed superimposition of metaphysical conceptuality and structure, threatens not only cross-cultural and cross-disciplinary interchange (it is evident in the dialogue concerning Mörike's poem) but even the essential conversation of "thinking ones." The source of the danger is the metaphysical understanding of the Differing that deploys the economy of philosophical discourse. An interlocution, however, can hope to be felicitous if it is willing to renounce strict conceptual determination, even allowing "that which is undeterminable" to slip away, while, at the same time, bringing it to unfold "its gathering power more and more radiantly" (GA 12, 95). Of course, such articulation is then in danger of being dismissed by those who seek to legislate the form of philosophically respectable discourse as unclear, needlessly complex, or at best "poetic."

The "voice" (*Stimme*, but emphatically not *phōnē*)[29] of that which "indeterminately determines" (*unbestimmtes Bestimmendes*) must, Heidegger insists, not be violently deflected or suppressed, even if this voice should turn out to be, as Tezuka notes, "silence itself" (GA 12, 106). The *logos*, which shelters what it brings to the radiance of its *phainesthai* back into essential concealment, must be allowed to come to word as what Heidegger, in another essay dating from 1950, "Die Sprache" (GA 12, 9–30),[30] called "the resounding of silence" (see chapter 2, below). In the context of the cross-cultural interchange between Heidegger and Tezuka, this "resounding of silence" is thematized from out of the Japanese understanding of art and, in particular, from out of Noh drama, as "hinting gesture" (*Wink, Gebärde*), which brings together the compelling phenomenal presencing of the singular as *iro* (color) with emptiness or vast sky (*kū*). What begins here to delineate itself in felicitous interlocution is an utterly remarkable chiasmatic inter-crossing of that which Heidegger likes to call the *essential* unsaid of Greek saying (in its relation to poetic articulation and to the closure of meta-physics) with Japanese language and thought.

Heidegger stresses that "the word," *logos*, which reverberates in the space of oscillation (*Schwingungsbereich*) of the Differing, is properly "hint" and not determination (*Bezeichnung*); "hinting" is "the fundamental trait of the word" (GA 12, 109). The hint as the reticent gesture enacted on the empty Noh stage evokes the particular in the enigma of its presencing and even in its grandeur (the example is a mountain chain), out of the non-phenomenal from which it remains undissevered. The hinting gesture here carries itself unto (*entgegentragen*) that which carries itself toward it (*zutragen*): great silence. In this sense, Heidegger characterizes *logos*, which is "hinting gesture," as "the gathering, originarily at one with itself, of carrying-unto and carrying-towards" (GA 12, 102). The emptiness of the carrying-toward, Tezuka observes, is "for us the highest name of what you [Heidegger] wish to say by the word 'Being' . . ." (GA 12, 103).

Since the word, *logos*, brings something into the radiant appearance of its phenomenal "color" (*iro*) by carrying it unto the vast emptiness of *kū*, *logos* is the saying-together of *iro* and *kū*, in close parallel to the ὁμολογεῖν . . . ἓν πάντα of Heraclitus (Fr. B 50) that Heidegger thematizes in "Logos."

Tezuka, at the outset of the interlocution, seeks to clarify Heidegger's understanding of hermeneutics and hermeneutic phenomenology, although, as the philosopher is quick to point out, these terms no longer appear in his later writings. The question, no sooner raised, is skirted and deferred; it cannot be addressed until the completion of the seeming detour through the hinting gesture and *iro/kū*. Only now can Heidegger present the notion of *hermeneuein* as indicating, not primarily a practice of interpretation, but "the bringing of tidings" of the "twofold" of Being and beings, or presenc-ing and what presences, in their "onefold," that is, of the Differing.

Hermeneuein is thus a name for the way in which mortal *legein* partici-pates responsively in *logos* understood as the saying-together of *hen/panta* or *iro/kū*. This sharing is not the imitation of some hypostatized *logos* (as surmised by those who charge Heidegger with "linguistic absolutism") but rather has its *essential* provenance in what Heidegger calls "the simple midst" between *legein* and *logos*,[31] which is the opening, the space of the clearing. In a quite similar sense, Tezuka answers Heidegger's question concerning the *essential* place (*Ort*) of a "deeply hidden kinship" that may exist between Japanese thought and that of Heidegger with the remark that the question reaches far into the distance, without limits, "which is shown to us in *kū*, which means the emptiness of the sky" (GA 12, 129).

The issue of hermeneutics was initially raised with reference to Shūzō Kuki, who, in his work *Iki no Kōzō*, struggled to elucidate the Japanese "aesthetic" notion of *iki* through the categories of a hermeneutical-phenomenological aesthetics.[32] A new avenue of approach has now been opened up, not only for rethinking *iki* but for clarifying the interrelation of *phainesthai, logos, poiēsis*, and beauty, which preoccupies Heidegger in his interchange with Staiger. Tezuka ventures a characterization of *iki* as "that which enchants" (*das Anmutende*),[33] being careful to dissociate the latter notion from the subject/object schema, from pleasure, stimulus, and the entire context of *aisthēsis* in which the cognate notion of beauty remains embedded. Heidegger also stresses the need to dissociate *Anmut* from Schiller's thematization and its formative influence on Hegel's aesthetics.

"That which enchants" is to be thought, instead, from out of the differential happening of manifestation, as the ravishing of "the silence which calls," as the sheer opening or clearing which releases presencing.

Only now can Tezuka respond to Heidegger's urgent request to speak the Japanese word—if such there is—which can answer to Heidegger's own non-metaphysical word for language: *die Sage*, "saying." The word that Tezuka ventures after much hesitation is *koto ba*. *Ba* seems to present no particular difficulties of interpretation; it indicates, according to Tezuka, falling petals, or perhaps, in a "translating" substitution, a donation of traces. *Koto*, which in this context has remained elusive, can now be interpreted as indicating that which comes forth out of *iki* (which is itself born from the counterplay of *iro* and *kū*), in such a manner that its mode of presencing is a bewitching enchantment:

> *Koto*, however, names that which, in the given instance, is itself what delights, that which uniquely in the unrepeatable moment comes to radiance (*Scheinen*) in the fullness of its enchantment. (Tezuka speaking; GA 12, 134)

In Mörike's Hegelian-metaphysical language, what announces itself here as *koto* is "was aber schön ist," that which presences in its beauty. This language, however, is not adequate to articulate Heidegger's concerns, for which reason the "other" which preoccupies him in the letters on Mörike must remain unnamed. The mere fact that the language is that of poetic articulation rather than of philosophical conceptuality does not free it from the oppression of its metaphysical burden. It is remarkable that Heidegger's concerns here can only be brought to word through the chiasmatic inter-crossing of non-metaphysical Japanese "saying" with the pre-metaphysical "saying" of ancient Greece.

It is Tezuka who, in an effort to forestall a metaphysical annexation of *iki*, returns immediately to the Greek fork of the chiasm, to the Sophoclean verse (*Aias*, v. 522) that Heidegger cites at the conclusion of his 1951 essay "Dichterisch wohnet der Mensch . . .": χάρις χάριν γάρ ἐστιν ἡ τίκτουσ ἀεί.[34]

Kharis, grace, enchantment, the analogue of *iki*, that which releases all presencing into its beauty without itself having any transcendent identity, is of itself *tiktousa*; it is "what properly poetizes, the surging source of the revealment of the twofold" (GA 12, 135). In that it poetizes, it is not sufficient unto itself but rather solicits mortal *legein* through which *phainesthai* comes to pass in historicity, and through which a place is prepared for the presencing of "what is beautiful" within the open "dimension" of human dwelling upon the earth. It is this question of enabling human dwelling which seems to prompt Heidegger's cryptic remark to Staiger, cited earlier, that the "other" which is at stake in the reading of Mörike's poem is what will decide "the relationship of language to us mortals."

Mortal *legein*, then, is poetic in *essence* as the donation of the traces of "what is beautiful," of the clear space of the opening. Through this donation the simplest of things, in the enchantment of their presencing, can open up and keep open the dimension of the enigma that is the dimension for human dwelling.

2

◆

Situating Heidegger
Situating Georg Trakl

The term poetry, applied to the least degraded
and least intellectualized forms of the expression
of a state of loss, can be considered synonymous
with expenditure; it in fact signifies, in the most
precise way, creation by means of loss.

Georges Bataille, "The Notion of Expenditure"

In the late 1930s, Heidegger begins to reach an understanding of technicity as the consummate articulation of the metaphysico-scientific-technical modality of un-concealment, whose salient traits are *absolutization* and *totalization* and which now holds sway as the frame-up of "posure" or *Ge-stell*.[1] *Poiēsis*, Heidegger insists, is essentially linked to technicity insofar as it is the differential, un-principled mode of articulation characteristic of *technē* in its ancient sense. With respect to language (which enables un-concealment), *poiēsis* is poetic articulation, which contrasts with the challenging-forth and the unconditional command characteristic of technicity. Since *poiēsis* remains mindful of the "mystery" or the lack of any inherent, positable reality in the happening of manifestation, it is able to awaken awareness of the destinal-historical ambiguity between totalizing and differential modalities of un-concealment in the *essence* of *Ge-stell*. By showing forth this ambiguity, *poiēsis* situates *Ge-stell* within an epochal destiny of manifestation that, in the manner appropriate to such a destiny (*Ge-schick*), perdures as a granting (*ge/währt*). As soon, however, as *Ge-stell* can be thus situated, we have gained what Heidegger calls a "free relationship" to it, so that its "entrapment" (*nachstellen*) of man's disclosive *essence* is foiled; and the extremity of "danger" becomes transmuted into "that which saves" by enabling an epochal turning.

13

The thinker's envisagement of such a turning is guided, for Heidegger, by the poet who, at the brink of nihilistic destitution, traces the trace of the withdrawal of the historical figures of divinity or the trace of "the holy" which is itself, on Heidegger's understanding, "the element of the trace."[2] This trace of the trace indicates no withheld presence or positivity but points, rather, to another, non-nihilistic way of experiencing and thinking the emptiness of "the abyss."

In seeking to follow the path traced out by the poet's nocturnal and estranged wandering, Heidegger implicitly contrasts the poet's guidance with another sort of guidance which had earlier enthralled him (not without an aura of spirituality): that of the political leader or *Führer* who, on his part—as was Heidegger's hybristic belief during his tenure of the rectorate of Freiburg University—required the thinker's spiritual and intellectual guidance.[3] The figure of the wandering poet who is "of another sense" and who has become a stranger to the contemporary cast (*Geschlecht*) of man (which itself is deeply estranged from man's disclosive *essence*) is not a figure capable of what Heidegger earlier called "spiritual legislation," but one who can trace out, in the depth of night, the uncertain itinerary of a possible transition.

The one poet who—as Heidegger reads him—lucidly discerns the horizon of his own age as one of spiritual desolation is Hölderlin. At the extremity of this desolation—the point where destitution masks itself with a plethora of needs clamoring insatiably for determinate satisfactions—Heidegger perceives the need for a "poetizing thinking" that lets itself be dialogically engaged by Hölderlin's problematizing of the very nature of poetic articulation. Given this understanding of the indispensability of Hölderlin's tracing guidance, Heidegger situates Trakl's poetry in the meteoric trail of Hölderlin's *Wirkungsgeschichte*, thereby recasting Trakl's own understanding of his Hölderlinian filiation.[4]

Heidegger's effort to accomplish a situating elucidation (*Erläuterung/Erörterung*) of Trakl's poetry sustains a double gesture: with one hand, so to speak, he welcomes and valorizes the upsurge of alterity and estrangement in the poetry; but with the other (and almost by a sleight of hand), he fits this alterity into an onto-historical vision and seeks to contain its disintegrative power. The second gesture of fitting containment inscribes a number of circles, each slightly decentered with respect to the others. Most prominent are the interpretive circle of elucidation and situation (centered in the "unsaid" proper to the saying), the circle of rejoining or retrieving, through *katabasis* and death, what has remained withheld or "unborn," and the circle which subtly interlinks poetic articulation with spirit (*Geist*) and pain. Since Trakl's poetry, given its disturbing, almost hallucinatory character, autumnal cadence, and thematization of disruption, decay, and disintegration, stubbornly resists the pacific serenity and perfection of the circle, Heidegger's sleight of hand conceals, at every move, a certain deformation of the poetry.

In examining Heidegger's dislocating situation and transforming elucidation of the poetry, our aim is not to restore to Trakl what might properly be his own. To do so would betray a flagrant disregard for the fact that the category of the proper is problematized both by Trakl's poetry of estrangement and by Heidegger's inseparable conjunction of appropriation with mortal dispropriation. The aim is rather to reveal the interpretive constraints and dynamics of Heidegger's reading, to situate this reading with respect to the exigencies which effract Heidegger's own "path of thinking," and the tensions which beset it. Our focus will be trained, in particular, on the figure of the wandering stranger and on the locality or "landscape," as Heidegger calls it, of his exile or wandering.

I

Heidegger seeks to situate Trakl's poetry at its "highest" and "most extreme" point of concentration or convergence, a gathering point always indicated by the individual poems but never reached. As the place of the surging forth and recollective convergence of the rhythmic flow of poetic saying, this gathering point *in extremis* remains dislocated into the unsaid. Heidegger insists that one must both elucidate individual poems by restoring them to their place in the unsaid and indicate this place, in turn, through the elucidation of individual poems. (GA 12, 33f). This circle of interpretation that interlinks the polarities of saying and the unsaid, of gathering and dispersion, requires that the plurivocity of Trakl's poetic diction should be referable to "an accord which, signified in itself, remains always unsayable." Plurivocity or multivalence is then not irreducible but constitutes, for Heidegger, an "ambiguous ambiguity," which is to say, one that can either be taken at face value or else understood, more perceptively, as the accord of "the severity of what releases" (GA 12, 71). This second understanding shows the unitary gathering point to be the place of un-principled, differential origination.

The move of letting the gathering point appear as the locus of dehiscence counteracts Heidegger's tendency, as a reader of poetry, to unwarranted unification—a tendency born of his understanding of poetry as what Kathleen Wright calls "composed concentration" and "excessive intensification."[5] It does not, however, keep him from carrying out an appropriative invasion and deformation of the poetry. Although he warns that, in addressing Trakl's poetry, the thinker must exercise particular restraint, he characteristically employs a strategy of fragmentation, wrenching words, verses, phrases, and even entire stanzas out of their contexts and re-connecting them to yield a thinker's poem resonant with the poet's voice. This work of fragmentation and re-assembly (which ignores the care Trakl himself devoted to arranging the sequence of his poems for publication[6]) masks the importance of rupture and negativity in Trakl's poetic sensibility, particularly in his thematization of estrangement.

Heidegger understands apartness (*Abgeschiedenheit*) as the "free domain" or "land" of the wandering stranger, which is situated in the "evening" of a decline (GA 12, 73). Since the locality (*Ortschaft*) of this site or place (*Ort*) is the still withheld "earliness," the promise or onto-historical destiny not yet brought to fruition, of the "land of evening" which is the Occident (*Abendland*), Heidegger understands the downward path of decline and perishing (*Untergang*) as an itinerary of transition (*Übergang*). Apartness as the domain of such a transition toward a new, matinal arising is marked out by the searching steps of the wandering stranger, who, far from being lost in errancy, prepares the way for living in mindfulness of the "mystery" of manifestation and in the practice of releasement. Apartness becomes the place of what Heidegger calls a poetic building and dwelling upon the earth.

In construing estrangement and wandering as a transition, Heidegger superimposes Hölderlin's understanding of the poet as a "swimmer," who, in abandoning himself to the perilous element, retrieves antiquity for his own time, upon Trakl's more conventional figure of the poet as wanderer.[7] This superimposition ignores the fact that wandering, unlike Hölderlin's "swimming," is not goal-directed but rather restless and random. Heidegger's forgetfulness of the contingency of all interpretation, which Wright stresses,[8] is thus markedly out of step with the errant wandering of Trakl's stranger.

The stranger, as Heidegger understands him, is "the departed one" (*der Abgeschiedene*) because he has parted from "the accursed cast" of man and has become "other for the others," namely, for the descendants of this decayed cast (*Geschlecht*; GA 12, 45f). His alterity and madness (*Wahnsinn*) appear, then, as a salutary "other" orientation (*Sinn*) to one who is prepared to abandon that of the decayed cast. The stranger's undoing and dying retrieves, for Heidegger, the promise of a "stiller childhood," which (in keeping with the plural meanings of *Geschlecht* as cast, tribe, family, or sex) assuages the divisive tensions that oppose man to nature and antagonize races and nations as well as the sexes. The wanderer's estrangement thus weaves, rather paradoxically, the bonds of reconciliation and prepares for a recasting of man which awaits "another arising." Reiner Schürmann, who interprets *Abgeschiedenheit*, in this context, as the practice of non-attachment, remarks:

> This is a somewhat contorted way of linking, beyond deconstruction, the arrival of an age that bears the mark of the originary (presencing freed

from the technological cathexis) to a return to the original dawn (ancient Greece).[9]

Such *Abgeschiedenheit* is not an apolitical retreat, for it gathers together those who follow the path of the wandering stranger in giving heed to the Differing and to un-principled poetic articulation, with a view to carrying to fruition the onto-historical destiny of the Occident.

This almost eschatological understanding of the stranger's itinerary, inspired by Heidegger's reading of Hölderlin, is nevertheless not Trakl's. Böschenstein has aptly remarked that Trakl, unlike Hölderlin, neither takes his bearings from a commemorated past nor envisages a future born from the retrieval of this past. Rather, both futurity and the past are "foreclosed in a single collapse."[10] This collapse is not a catastrophic or an apocalyptic event; it is rather an autumnal devastation and disintegration. Böschenstein points out that Hölderlin and Rimbaud, the major formative influences on Trakl's poetry, are not progressively reconciled in his poetic development but are brought together only through a relentless transposition into negativity. Through the challenges of a persistent counter-word, or *Widerruf*, Trakl, according to Böschenstein, subverts both Hölderlin's Dionysian "joyful madness" and "a largely intact and often nearly intoxicated, indeed ecstatic" dimension in Rimbaud. This subversion opens upon a nocturnal and autumnal poetic landscape in which the marks of the familiar become undecipherable, and which is caught up in "speechless mourning."

The figure of the stranger is, for Trakl, one not of salutary apartness and expectant transition but of disruption. Although the stranger appears in historical and legendary guises (Elis, Kaspar Hauser, Sebastian) as the poet's alter-ego, the figure is also transposed into the feminine or the indefinite neuter (*ein Fremdes*); and it appears ambiguously as both criminal and guiltless, dead, murdered, or unborn. The stranger in the guises of the "white son," the "double," the "radiant corpse," the "young novice," or the seer afflicted with madness appears frequently in the reflected or autoscopic image, which is prone to sudden and terrifying disfiguration or disintegration (as, for instance, in *Traum und Umnachtung*). Russell Brown points out that Trakl resorts to traditional and naive pastoral motives only to shock and disorient the reader's expectations by his "bizarre explosions."[11] Although Brown's emphasis on irony and wit in Trakl's subversion of the familiar sounds a neglected note in Trakl studies, one must heed also Trakl's poignant and irresoluble tensions between the beauty of a serene ancestral order (which nevertheless masks violence) and the affliction and exile of the (de)parted one.

Böschenstein shows that the ghostly figure of Daedalus functions, for Trakl, as a cipher for Hölderlin's poetic paternity, although Hölderlin sometimes appears fraternally in the poems as the singing brother of "exalted destiny." With respect to the ghost of Daedalus, Trakl's protagonist is Icarus, the fallen son whose ruin and dying mark the failure of soaring poetic aspirations.[12] The fifth and final version of Trakl's poem "Untergang," dedicated to another afflicted poet brother, Karl Borromäus Heinrich, deserves to be cited here in its entirety:

> Über den weissen Weiher
> sind die wilden Vögel fortgezogen.
> Am Abend weht von unseren Sternen ein eisiger Wind.
>
> Über unsere Gräber
> beugt sich die zerbrochene Stirne der Nacht,
> Unter Eichen schaukeln wir auf einem silbernen Kahn.
>
> Immer klingen die weissen Mauern der Stadt.
> Unter Dornenbogen
> O mein Bruder klimmen wir blinde Zeiger gen Mitternacht.[13]

This poem shows clearly that it is the very path of ascent, the path of poetic intensity and exaltation, which leads toward loss and perishing, whereas Heidegger's path, the path of the thinker, traverses decline and darkness in search of another arising. For Trakl, the soaring ascent of Daedalus and Icarus under the high sun has become an agonized climb toward midnight; the poets, as "blind pointers," cannot, in the darkness, provide guidance for a momentous historical transition.

II

The path of Trakl's stranger, as Heidegger traces it, is a spiritual path; it leads through spiritual (*geistlicher*) darkness toward the holy, symbolized by the color blue. The constellation of spirit, flame, soul, and pain (perhaps a non-pacific articulation of the Fourfold) forms the encrypted core of Heidegger's meditation. Although these encrypted notions mesh easily with Trakl's poetic vocabulary, they enable Heidegger to integrate his exegesis of Trakl with his reading of Hegel, Schelling, and Hölderlin. This is especially true—as Derrida has noted—of the notion and the whole problematic of spirit.[14] Through Trakl's choice of adjective (*geistlich* rather than *geistig*), *Geist* is freed of its usual ambivalence between "mind" and "spirit" and weighted decisively toward the latter sense. Heidegger's thematization of spirit remains, ultimately, not only cryptic but crypto-political; as Derrida suggests, the thematic of *Geist* "perhaps even decides the sense of the political as such."[15]

Heidegger, rejecting any mentalistic, dualistic, or dialectical metaphysics of spirit, understands *Geist* as a flaming wind, indicating, by this pentecostal and Hölderlinian trope, the driven *ec-stasis* (*Ausser-sich*) and effractive passion of man's *essence*. *Geist* as a flaming wind (one can discern, in the remote distance, the Heraclitean *prēstēr*) is both illuminating and consuming, and Heidegger thematizes these dual possibilities as "the gathering coming-into-flower of the gentle" and as the flagrancy of deluded passion which ignites the conflagration of evil (see GA 12, 56). Not only are both flagrant evil and the sort of manifestation which Heidegger calls *scheinen* (shining, understood here in a trans-phenomenological sense) essential possibilities for the kinetic momentum of spirit, but they are both equally nourished by the "flame" which soul entrusts to spirit and which in turn enables spirit to be the bestower of life and soul (GA 12, 56–58). Heidegger speaks of this flame of the soul in Trakl's idiom as "glowing melancholy," or, in his own words, as "all-pervading pain" (GA 12, 64). This pain which is the "trait" and passion of the soul, as well as "the Being-character of all that is in Being" (*die Gunst des Wesenhaften alles Wesenden*), bespeaks the dispossession which characterizes mortal existence—an inherent lack that Plato (for whom the driving and ambiguous passion was not spirit but *erōs*) compellingly thematized.

Pain, according to Heidegger, is the motivating truth of evil, but it can also motivate an enlightened understanding of the character of manifestation. What characterizes the spiritual dynamics of evil is a relentless, deluded pull or draw (*Fortriss*), which rivets individuals as well as entire populations and historical periods to the pursuit of absolutization and totalization. The "singeing" (*sengende*) wildness of this relentless pull is the curse that weighs upon the "accursed cast" of man, the cast that, in the grip of technicity, is heedless of mortality and intolerant of differentiation. This cast or *Geschlecht* proceeds to make sexual, racial, ideological, or national differences the occasion for antagonistic opposition, rupture, singularization and disintegration. Heidegger marks the emergence of the decayed cast and destinal curse (*Schlag*, the root of *Geschlecht*) out of the ambivalent dynamics of spirit in a way which can barely be approximated in English, through the contrast between *zerschlagen* (to shatter) and *verschlagen* (to transpose).

The other cast or standpoint is that of enlightened vision (as it may well be called, given the spiritualization of Heidegger's vocabulary), which allows the *Fortriss* driven by pain (the unrecognized pull of the Differing at the heart of manifestation) to be checked and stilled by the countermovement of a backward pull or *Rückriss* that brings the dynamic intensities into equipoise and transforms singeing wildness into a "flaming regard." The latter, Heidegger believes, is brought to voice and resounds in the poet's singing (*singen*, as both linked to and contrasted with *sengen*). Through the double pull of *Fortriss* and *Rückriss*, the "great soul" is brought to a standpoint where it responds receptively to the double, if not duplicitous, movement of the holy, the movement of the trace which is Being's self-withdrawing bestowal. Heidegger, appropriating Trakl's imagery and diction, calls this movement of the holy "the brightness sheltered into the dark," or speaks of it as the somber luminosity of the color blue (GA 12, 40). Through being irradiated with blueness, the radiance of the holy, the wildness of human existence is calmed and its pain "stilled" without being assuaged. The thinking and acting of the cast of man characterized by "blue" rather than "singeing" wildness (a cast which is still horizonal) are marked by the practice of non-attachment or of a releasement which is not dispassionate.

Apartness, *Abgeschiedenheit*, as the "place" of a gathering into estrangement, namely, into the non-dissembled strangeness of mortal existence, is itself, Heidegger remarks, "clarified spirit" ("der lautere Geist"; GA 12, 62); as such it can accomplish what Trakl calls "the transmutation of evil." The "powerful pain" of mortality, restrained by the backward pull into apartness from expressing itself as destructive wildness, becomes, according to Heidegger, the guardian of those who are of an enlightened spiritual cast; and such guardianship consigns them to the casting of a *Geschlecht* of man which is still to come. This cast, given its oblique relation to the decayed cast, can come into its own at the closure of principial economies of presencing ("restricted economies," as Derrida calls them, in the vocabulary of Bataille). Heidegger describes this cast, in Trakl's poetic language, as at once "dead" and "unborn," namely, as promised and prepared for but withheld and not brought to fruition in the "archic" or principial configurations of presencing.

Since apartness, for Heidegger, is at once clarified spirit and the source which originates and regathers Trakl's "unsaid poem," the question arises of how it can "bring a poetic saying and singing underway."

The poet, according to Heidegger, is one who listens after "the departed one," the figure of spiritual transition. He responds to the footsteps of this wanderer "with the bird-voice of the deathlike one," which sings also the perishing of the decayed cast of man (GA 12, 65). In following the steps of the departed one, the poet himself (for Heidegger the poet is always gendered in the masculine) becomes a wandering stranger. Since apartness, as the locality of his wandering, "is in the manner of its flaming itself spirit, and as such that which gathers" (GA 12, 63), he is able to let apartness exert its draw through his poetic articulation. Others are thus enabled to enter into the draw, and the poet becomes, as already noted, a guide who repudiates the sort of leadership characteristic of the configuration of *Fortriss*.

The notion of spirit that pertains here to the encrypted core of Heidegger's meditation is crucial also to his rectoral address of 1933 in its concern with the self-assertion or autonomy of the German university.[16] In one of his retrospective attempts at self-justification, Heidegger writes, in 1945, that it was his aim, in accepting the rectorate, to effect a spiritual transformation "from within National Socialism and in relation to it"—a transformation not merely of the structure of the university (or of the institutionalization of knowledge) but one, ultimately, which responds to the spiritual crisis and reverses the decline of the West. He notes that he saw the thought of such a transformation as a challenge to the National Socialist position that "spirit and the spiritual world are merely an expression of racial givens."[17]

Heidegger, then, understood his assumption of the rectorate essentially as an election and commitment to spiritual leadership—a leadership which derives its privilege from a discerning attunement to "the spiritual mission that forces the destiny of the German people to bear the stamp of its history."[18] Under the rectifying guidance of the rector, the university is to leave behind both the distressingly "disintegrated multiplicity" of the intellectual disciplines and the totalizing model of unification provided by their politization under the aegis of *politische Wissenschaft*. It is to become, instead, "a place of spiritual legislation" that hearkens back to the "distant command" of the Greek beginnings of Western thought.

The importance of this beginning lies, according to Heidegger, in the fact that it treated *questioning*, the "ungrounded holding of one's ground in the midst of the uncertainty of the entirety of what is," as the highest form of knowing. The "spiritual mission" that ties the German people to this beginning is to be understood as their willingness to expose themselves, in their thinking and their pursuit of knowledge, to "the fertility and the blessing bestowed by all the world-shaping powers of human-historical *Dasein*," that is, to place themselves unprotected into the open.[19] As Wright points out, the "Fatherland," for Heidegger, is "the historical Being of a (here the German) people," which is to say, its spiritual destiny "founded" by the poet and "instituted" by the thinker.[20] As Heidegger remarked to Karl Löwith in 1936 (when he lectured in Rome on "Hölderlin and the Essence of Poetry"), his politics sprang from and reflected his understanding of historicity (*Geschichtlichkeit*);[21] and his thought of historicity is indissociable from that of the spiritual destiny of Germany and the Occident.

Despite the emphasis on ungrounded openness, spirit, as Heidegger understands it in his rector's address and in related contexts, has a powerfully integrative and unifying function: it not only ties the resolution of a contemporary crisis to the mandate of Greek antiquity, but it also constrains those who are in a position of "following" (the student body of the university and, ultimately, the people at large) to accept the leadership (*Führerschaft*) of those capable of discerning Germany's spiritual destiny. Furthermore, it brings together the three forms of service to the nation that Heidegger distinguishes (by labor, arms, and knowledge) into "one formative force" and breaks down the departmental divisions of the university. In doing so, however, it supposedly safeguards the differential articulation of what it unifies, as distinct from the totalizing unification effected by the politization of the intellectual disciplines (*staatliche Wissenschaft*).

The main difference between the two meditations on spirit is that Heidegger abandons his earlier identification of spirit with the historical destiny or historical world of a people, and thinks spirit as pure *ec-stasis* with two essential (and therefore indissociable) possibilities. Since the *ec-stasis* is sustained by the "pain" of mortality (the "flame" of ambiguous power which "soul" entrusts to spirit), it both "lightens and lets [things] shine forth in radiance . . . [and] can go on devouring and reducing everything to the whiteness of ash" GA 12, 56). Whereas spirit as historical configuration is thought in wholly positive, indeed, salvific terms, spirit thought as *ec-stasis* cannot accomplish "the gathering of the gentle," which is differential unification, unless its dynamism becomes the counter-movement of *Fortriss* and *Rückriss*. Through the backward pull (*Rückriss*), "all-pervasive pain" realizes its inapparent responsive relationship to the "blueness" (the inward-gathering and stilling power) of the holy, which latter is for Heidegger not an onto-theological notion but the element of the trace. In every flaming in-spiration, there threatens the other possibility, that of evil (*das Böse*), which is "the uproar of what un-settles (*des Ent-setzenden*), flaming forth into a blindness that displaces (*versetzt*) into the ungatheredness of the unsalutary" (GA 12, 156). It appears that the *ec-stasis* that transposed the thinker into the political arena would now itself be situated under the sign of sheer *Fortriss*.

The threshold which divides these essential possibilities of spirit is tenuous, and Heidegger, in both his essays on Trakl, devotes considerable attention to the trope of the petrified threshold in the third stanza of Trakl's "Ein Winterabend":

> Wanderer tritt still herein;
> Schmerz versteinerte die Schwelle.
> Da erglänzt in reiner Helle
> Auf dem Tische Brot und Wein.[22]

The petrification of the threshold, as Heidegger understands it, is the "petrification" or adamantine solidification of pain itself, in virtue of which pain safeguards the Differing against the rampant pull of totalizing inspiration. Heidegger's appropriative gesture of interpretation here leads him into some farfetched and implausible construals, such as treating the *da* in the cited stanza as locative (hence locating bread and wine on the threshold), or reading a verse from "Heiterer Frühling" ("Truly! I shall be with you always") which evidently cites the religious inscription on a gravestone, as the very voice of petrified pain. Nevertheless, the turn of thought that, in its concern with the spiritual and intellectual nature of evil and its blinding power, mandates these torsions is powerful and clear.

The thinker here is no longer called upon to "institute" what the poet has "founded"; he is required only to follow the poet's footfall into a nocturnal wandering. Heidegger's stress on the conventional trope of the poet as wanderer calls attention to his new conception of the poet's (and the thinker's) guidance as neither goal-directed nor practically efficacious in foreseeable ways. Instead, he thinks of such guidance as a groping and daring transition to a new intellectual and spiritual vantage point or place of abiding. Although such a transformation of thinking neither can nor need be "applied" in *praxis*, it alone—such is now Heidegger's conviction—offers the possibility of a far-reaching transformation of *praxis*.[23]

For Heidegger, the "place" for such an alteration of thinking remains language; and for this reason his expectancy of such an advent must dislocate its own articulation into the straits of an interlocution (*Zwiesprache*) between poet and thinker that is not a dialogical exchange between two intact subjectivities but one in which both are dispropriated. The nature and role of language in this dispropriating *Gespräch* must therefore become the final focus for the present chapter.

<h1 style="text-align:center">III</h1>

Heidegger insists that language is no human doing, nor the representation or expression of thought and feeling, but that man himself appears, within the "speaking of language" ("das Sprechen der Sprache"), as a *Versprechen*, which is to say, as both a promise or commitment and a mis-speaking.[24] This ambiguity is the very ambiguity of *poiēsis* or bringing forth into unconcealment; its opposite yet always meridinally interconnected poles are the unconditional command of totalizing provocation and a poetic articulation that allows (wo)man to fulfill his/her highest calling, which is "to guard the unconcealedness, and together with it always first the concealedness, of all beings (*Wesen*) upon this earth."[25] By turning to the poets, one can therefore hope to enter into what Heidegger calls a "free relation" to the *essence* of technicity. Instead of understanding technicity in its own terms (as a means, or as neutral power), one will then understand it in its ambiguity which bespeaks the ambiguous nature of un-concealment, of truth (FT, 5–7, 33).

How does Trakl's poetic articulation, his very diction, show the aspect of *poiēsis* which safeguards the enigma of manifestation? Heidegger, in keeping with his distressing tendency to neglect *lexis*, does not explicitly address this question. One can indicate here that, in Trakl's poetic articulation, the place of the subject, together with the subject-predicate structure characteristic of Indo-Germanic languages, is relentlessly crossed out and rendered indecidable. This does not happen (as in Celan's poetry) through a dismemberment and "dissemination" of language itself, but rather through poetic resources which include the juxtaposition of antagonistic figures and imagery without mediation and resolution, constant shifts of perspective which frustrate any effort to locate and define the figures, and a heightening of ambiguity through the use of tenuous subjunctive constructions and of conjunctions which convey uncertainty or plural possibilities. By recourse to such poetic resources, Trakl transposes the familiar into an uncanny and dreamlike dimension and maintains a precarious balance between corrosive disintegration and transfiguration.

Böschenstein points out that Hölderlin's influence (which becomes more pronounced during Trakl's final years, 1912–14) shows itself above all in the syntax and rhythm of Trakl's diction, but that the poet, at the same time, subjects Hölderlin's hymnic diction to a relentless fragmentation and ellipsis.[26] Trakl thus not only frustrates the reader's linguistic habitualities (which insinuate absolutization) but also marks the resistances of a "speechless" refusal and of the unsayable, which is to say, that he articulates mortality.

For Heidegger, the site or essential place of language is the place of a "gathering into *Ereignis*," the locus of manifestation opened up through ungrounded poetic configuration (*tiktein, dichten*). Such configuration commends what it commands or mandates to stand forth into manifestation to the rift of the Differing, the articulating "threshold" which intimately conjoins "world" (here a name for the fourfold mirror-play of presencing) and "things," while also keeping them strictly parted, without possible con-fusion. This conjoining yet parting threshold is pain, because, in its implacable "stoniness," it repudiates the human desire for comprehensive unification and grounding. By its resistance to all ruses of reification, to the ascriptions of inherent reality, and to the gestures of in-different totalization, the gathering into dif-ference which happens through poetic language is able to stem the pull of *Fortriss* and to still its wildness. In allowing stillness (which is not dispassionate quiescence) to mark the very heart of manifestation, language becomes what Heidegger calls "*das* Geläut der Stille," roughly translatable as "the resounding of stillness." This phrase, which makes its appearance near the end of "Die Sprache," says the same as the initial phrase describing language as the "gathering into *Ereignis*," but it is also its chiasmatic and completing inversion:

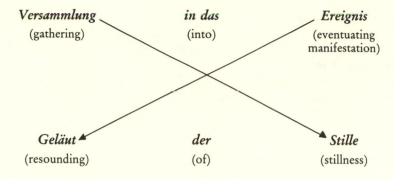

Versammlung	in das	Ereignis
(gathering)	(into)	(eventuating manifestation)
Geläut	der	Stille
(resounding)	(of)	(stillness)

In this chiasmatic structure, the gathering achieves stillness, whereas *Geläut* announces the events of manifestation insofar as these (due to their relation to gathering and stillness) refuse the *adikia* (in the language of Anaximander) of self-absolutization.

Heidegger's insistence that "die Sprache spricht" does not bespeak linguistic mysticism or absolutism, but rather, it makes the precise point that linguistic articulation, as such or most properly, commends what it mandates into manifestation to the Differing, in that, as ungrounded configuration, it is "essentially poetic." There is here a subtle play of irony (a generally overlooked trait of Heidegger's discourse), in that what is most proper to language or to human speaking is a thoroughgoing dispropriation. In virtue of this dispropriation, (wo)man, the speaker, is a *Versprechen* of language, consigned and promised to the Differing, yet unable to sustain this promise due to his or her passionate and consuming pursuit of what is mis-spoken as the "ownmost."

Heidegger cautions that the commending command of language has indeed become almost inaudible in the economy of everyday discourse, where language functions as a mere token of exchange. It remains discernible only in what he calls "the purely spoken" ("das rein Gesprochene"). He uses the past participle here (as in his standard phrase *das Gewesene*) in an Hegelian manner to indicate not the occasion of a lost innocence but a present speaking that has fully come into its own in exercising its "essencing and whiling" or (in perhaps now more familiar language) its commending command. What is "purely spoken" then is the poem which responds to and bespeaks the lucid spirit of apartness.

Such speaking, nevertheless, is displaced into a pastness incapable of ever being brought to immediacy and presence, because it can be articulated and heard only on the way, in the temporal distension and non-fulfillment of itineracy. The path of this wandering, as Heidegger understands it, seeks a (de)parted homecoming. The "home" in question is not some homey idyll, any more than Heidegger's "earth" indicates an agrarian utopia. Rather, the ironic notions of "home" and "earth" indicate a mortal dwelling marked by the practice of releasement.

Since (de)parted homecoming is the effraction of a way, it articulates its double partedness from what it has taken leave of as well as from what it continues to seek. What is sought for can then be indicated only with reference to what has been abandoned. The language of the purely spoken is a language of the in-between, the interval, the twilight. What belongs to the interval cannot be appropriated but only inter-rogated. The thinker must encounter the twilight language of the purely spoken in the in-between, in the dispropriation of *Zwiesprache* or interlocution. A certain ambiguity or double gesture will, indeed, characterize such *Zwiesprache*, the interlocution between poetizing and thinking into whose uncharted straits Heidegger dislocates his own meditation.

Heidegger begins and ends his *Zwiesprache* with Trakl's poetry by addressing parts of the poem "Frühling der Seele," which Trakl placed near the end of his last collection of poetry, *Sebastian im Traum*, published posthumously in 1915. Quite characteristically, Heidegger does not consider the poem as a whole but begins with a meditation on a single verse and contents himself, at the end, with citing the penultimate and last strophes, which he regards as "the ascent of the song into the pure melodious sound of the spiritual years through which the stranger wanders" (GA 12, 77), by way of a conclusion to his own study.

A reading of the poem in its entirety remains desirable both as an avenue of approach to Trakl's poetic articulation and as a way of tracing, in part, the double gesture of Heidegger's interpretation.

Frühling der Seele

Aufschrei im Schlaf; durch schwarze Gassen stürzt der Wind,
Das Blau des Frühlings winkt durch brechendes Geäst,
Purpurner Nachttau und es erlöschen rings die Sterne.
Grünlich dämmert der Fluss, silbern die alten Alleen
Und die Türme der Stadt. O sanfte Trunkenheit
Im gleitenden Kahn und die dunklen Rufe der Amsel
In kindlichen Gärten. Schon lichtet sich der rosige Flor.

Feierlich rauschen die Wasser. O die feuchten Schatten der Au,
Das schreitende Tier; Grünendes, Blütengezweig
Rührt die kristallene Stirne; schimmernder Schaukelkahn.
Leise tönt die Sonne im Rosengewölk am Hügel.
Gross ist die Stille des Tannenwalds, die ernsten Schatten am Fluss.

Reinheit! Reinheit! Wo sind die furchtbaren Pfade des Todes,
Des grauen steinernen Schweigens, die Felsen der Nacht
Und die friedlosen Schatten? Strahlender Sonnenabgrund.

Schwester, da ich dich fand an einsamer Lichtung
Des Waldes und Mittag war und gross das Schweigen des Tiers;
Weisse unter wilder Eiche, und es blühte silbern der Dorn.
Gewaltiges Sterben und die singende Flamme im Herzen.

Dunkler umfliessen die Wasser die schönen Spiele der Fische.
Stunde der Trauer, schweigender Anblick der Sonne;
Es ist die Seele ein Fremdes auf Erden. Geistlich dämmert
Bläue über dem verhauenen Wald und es läutet
Lange eine dunkle Glocke im Dorf; friedlich Geleit.
Stille blüht die Myrthe über den weissen Lidern des Toten.

Leise tönen die Wasser im sinkenden Nachmittag
Und es grünet dunkler die Wildnis am Ufer, Freude im rosigen
    Wind;
Der sanfte Gesang des Bruders am Abendhügel.[27]

The poem's dramatic opening verse, with its somber assonance, sibilant alliteration, and accelerating rhythm, plunges the reader into a nightmare scene of nocturnal terror and desolation. As the sleeper wakens in the gliding boat, however, there unfolds a densely woven tapestry of calmer images, some of which, such as the breaking branches, the crimson night-dew, and the extinguished stars, still recall the nocturnal scene, whereas others are matinal and vernal. Characteristically, Trakl leaves this contrast irresolvable. The "breaking branches," in particular, show how Trakl achieves indecidability through a displacement of the adjective: the branches break up the blue dawn sky; but at the same time the position of the adjective suggests their breakage in the nightmare's plunging wind. In the remainder of the stanza, the metrical shifts and, in particular, the use of hovering accent in the fifth and seventh verses, together with the insistent repetition of the vowels *u*, *ü*, and *i*, create a calming and slowing effect and suggest the rocking motion and iridescent "shimmering" of the boat. The figure of the boat in Trakl's poetry—the "silver," "blackish," or "anxious" boat—can be understood as an autofiguration of his art.

Whereas Heidegger, by citing only the last two strophes of the poem, thematizes twilight and evening as the "locality" of a wandering which seeks a new arising out of the Occident's decline (thus conjoining *Untergang* and *Übergang*), the poem, in fact, follows the itinerary of a river journey from pre-dawn darkness to an ecstatic experience at high noon, and finally through the "hour of mourning" into hesperian gentleness. No circle is completed, for to close the circle would mean a return to sheer nightmare.

Whereas the atmosphere created in the first strophe is fresh and vernal, the second strophe, with its hymnic cadence and Dantesque image of the sun rising over a hill, carries a tone of solemn majesty. The "earnest shadows," the "striding animal," and the somber spruces are arrayed like ceremonial witnesses to an imminent transfiguration. In keeping with the plural meanings of *rühren*, the "crystal forehead" of the protagonist is not only "touched" but also moved and, like an instrument, caused to sound forth by the young leaves and flower-branches, while the risen sun itself "softly resounds." The emphasis on pure, exalted sound and the connotation of the poet's crown in the figure of the "crystal" forehead touched by the branches and leaves supports the suggestion that the thematic concern of the poem is poetry itself—not, as Heidegger thinks it, in relation to the historical destiny of the West, but in the context of the poet's errant life journey.

The moment of transfiguration and transport seems about to be reached with the ecstatic invocation of purity which opens the third strophe. However, at the threshold of exalted inspiration and poetic rapture, the protagonist must recall the banished terrors of death, "stony silence," (stoniness, for Trakl, is refusing and menacing rather than firm and calm, as Heidegger reads it), and the turbulence of the nightmare scene. The moment of realization is thus not mystically lifted out of time; it shows the work of memory and is infiltrated by what it seeks to hold in abeyance. Instead of undertaking the return to a withheld "earliness," which Heidegger emphasizes, the protagonist is obsessively haunted by the return of banished violence, confusion, and terror.

The visionary realization is consummated in the fourth strophe, which is set in the exalted stillness of high noon. Instead of any cosmic, religious, historical, or even artistic vision, however, it is the sister who appears; and the place of this at once familiar and unearthly epiphany is a solitary forest clearing, a place remote from human habitation and interpretation. The sudden shift from an utterly impersonal mode of discourse to the first person singular suggests that the protagonist locates and finds himself only in finding the sister in her enigmatic remoteness. The opening verses of this strophe are almost bereft of punctuation and, with breathless intensity, run together, the clearing, the noon hour, the animal's silence, and above all the "I" and "you" (*ich dich*). The white figure of the sister appears at once infrangibly remote and so compellingly close as to effect an almost hallucinatory redoubling of the self, which affects it with alterity. The moments of alterity and sameness keep referring to one another in an abyssal iteration which contaminates any transfiguration and which (*pace* Heidegger) emphasizes the rift of sexual difference.

The narrative sentence that begins with *da* in the first verse remains incomplete; what ensues is not simply the straightforward consummation of illicit love as an episode in ordinary time. Rather, the "vehement dying" which kindles "the singing flame in the heart" alters the very order and temporality of experience; it is this altered order which is the order of the poem. In joining himself to the "white one under wild oak," through the silver flowering of the black and wounding thorn, the poet (now identified with the protagonist) becomes the "dead one," parted from the ancestral order no less than from what may be the degeneracy of the age, and given to errant wandering.

In the fifth strophe, the blinding intensity of the noon hour has yielded to the bereaved "hour of mourning." The ambiguity of the genitive in "schweigender Anblick der Sonne" suggests that silence afflicts the sun itself no less than the poet who gazes into its abyssal radiance. Out of this twofold silence and refusal—rather than out of a Heideggerian experience of departed homecoming—and with the halting awkwardness of inverted word order and an almost stammering repetition of the vowel *e*, Trakl voices the realization that the soul is "something strange upon earth." Silence and estrangement, however, do not prepare for the dawn of another arising.

In this solar silence and refusal, Trakl's protagonist, nevertheless, is accompanied far into the distance by the dark tolling of the village bell, which marks the meaningful order of life from which his dying has parted him. The "spiritual" blueness which spreads over the mutilated forest cannot undo or heal the mutilation, but it encompasses and soothes it. The poet's crown of fresh leaves and flowers has now become a crown of white-flowering myrtle, at once bridal and funereal. The myrtle, flower of classical antiquity, adorns the dead and sightless one's white eyelids while at the same time honoring his song (given the play on the homonyms *Lider/Lieder*), but it also links him both to the white sister in her apartness and to the "singing brother upon the evening hill," the figure of Hölderlin as the poet who retrieves Greek antiquity. It is worth noting that the relation between brother and sister has here become triplicitous, rather than striving, as Heidegger understands it, for the unification of a twofold.

In the poem's final strophe, it is gentle song, the very art of the poet, rather than any essential-historical vision which could be shared and brought into its own by the philosopher, that promises reconciliation and even (with an echo of the initial matinal images) "joy in the rosy wind." The subtle craft of the poem—the craft (to play on the boat image) of its *lexis* rather than of any encrypted or unconsummated meaning, its fragile and enigmatic self-sufficiency—is what the poet at last gives himself over to. Heidegger, however, remains reluctant thus to entrust himself, and his call for interlocution is, at least in part, a safeguard against the siren song that invites entrustment.

3

◆

The Sphere and the Ball: Rilke's (Dis)figuration

Zwischen dir und dem Land entsteht eine eisige Bindung—
So liege, werde jünger und fliege, unendlich dich geradebiegend.
Sie sollen dich nicht fragen, die Jungen, die Künftigen,—jene—
Wie es dir geht dort—in der Leere, in der Reinheit—dir, dem Waisen!

From a requiem poem for Ossip Mandelstamm by Andrej Belyi; trans.
Ralph Dutli

Between you and the land there comes to be an icy bond—
So lie there, become younger and fly, infinitely bending yourself into straightness.
They shall not ask you, the young ones, the ones still to come,—those—
how you are faring there—in emptiness, in purity—you, the orphan!

HEIDEGGER, PARMENIDES, RILKE

In his lecture course on Parmenides, offered in 1942/43,[1] Heidegger counter-poses his own understanding of the Open, as indicated by Parmenides's "trans-posing word"[2] *alētheia*, to Rilke's thought of the Open in the *Eighth Duino Elegy*. He criticizes Rilke's poetic thought as a late form of "modern metaphysics in the sense of secularized Christianity," which evinces "the spirit of Schopenhauer's philosophy as transmitted by Nietzsche and the doctrines of psychoanalysis" (GA 54, 235). Specifically, Heidegger both delineates and objects to a Rilkean reversal, which, in supposed rebellion against metaphysical hierarchy, privileges the figure of the animal and of unreflective "creation" over human subjectivity by granting it immediate and perhaps exclusive access to the Open. Such a reversal, he finds, succeeds only in reassigning established relative positions while continuing to affirm

30

and maintain the hierarchical, polarized, and representational schemata of metaphysical reason.

Against the background of this critique, Heidegger strives to articulate a trans-metaphysical thinking which reveals the temporality of manifestation as a topology of destinal belonging (GA 54, 210). For such a thinking, the visual and light metaphorics of the Western tradition points to an unconsummated original experience of the Open as the domain of manifestation permeated by the "divine glance," which solicits man's responsive glance (GA 54, 219).[3] Since the figure of man is here no longer thought metaphysically and humanistically, but rather with respect to the Open and the tensional character of *alētheia*, a "revolution" of thinking which seeks to erase the face of man becomes unnecessary.

Although one may have reservations about Heidegger's need, in the intellectual and political context of these lectures, to construe Nietzsche's thought and Rilke's poetry and poetics as a rejected Other, so as to gain the momentum for his own thinking, one must acknowledge the justice of his observation that a humanizing elevation of animal life (he speaks of the emergence of the figure of the animal as a sort of "overman") misses "the essential boundary between the mystery of living beings . . . and the mystery of what is historical." It is, of course, the latter "mystery" which engages Heidegger's thought. Refusing an "animalizing" of man (as *animal rationale*) no less than a humanizing of animal existence, he remarks profoundly that to divine "what lies hidden in living beings" requires a poetic sensibility and gifts of an order which may be as yet unrealized (GA 54, 239).

Throughout this discussion, Heidegger approaches Rilke's poetry in the same way as he reads Parmenides's fragmentary philosophical poem or the Heraclitean fragments: as a poetic modality of thinking that articulates itself chiefly through its deployment of certain key words which call for the thinker's reflective analysis. Although Heidegger disclaims any ability to offer a "precise delimitation" of important Rilkean words such as "creation" (*die Kreatur*) or "the Open" (*das Offene*), let alone to carry out a full interpretation of the *Duino Elegies* (GA 54, 229), he trusts his own meditation on "basic words" to give him access to Rilke's poetry and to reveal its organizing thought-structures.

Barely four years later, in the labored and difficult essay "What Are Poets For?",[4] Heidegger points to the fact that Rilke's poetry problematizes its own language, or "saying," as an indication of its at least partial resistance to the metaphysical-technical configuration. He insists that "saying," as the element of the trace, constitutes both the "sacred precinct" (*Bezirk, templum*) of Being and the transgressive reach of the "greater daring," which, as a "breath about nothing," exceeds the constraints not only of metaphysical logic but also of its inversion, the "logic of the heart." Whereas the Parmenides lectures located Rilke's poetry unambiguously and rather unceremoniously within the closure of metaphysics, the later essay achieves resolution neither concerning Rilke's role as a poet in a destitute time nor concerning his relationship to what, in the language of Paul Celan but in the spirit of Heidegger, one can call Hölderlin's "unsurpassable prescript."

The irresolution reflects at least in part the fact that, although Heidegger's problematic has developed and gained sharper focus, his method of approaching the poetry remains unchanged. What is now at issue for Heidegger, as already indicated, is the poet's own problematizing of his vocation and, ultimately, of his poetic articulation; for this is taken to be the distinguishing mark of a poetry responsive to a destitute time. Heidegger, however, continues to address this issue by interrogating the "fundamental words" (*Grundworte*) of what he takes to be Rilke's "valid poetry" (albeit the poem on which his interpretation focuses is, curiously, one that Rilke had composed as a dedication and described as "improvised verses"; *Holzwege* (hereinafter HW), 255). Given his appropriation of Hölderlin's "experience of history," Heidegger seeks in Rilke's "basic words" an awareness that what lacks wholeness and salutary or even salvific power (*das Heillose*) is the effaced trace of the trace which he describes as "the holy" (*das Heilige*). Within the holy as the element of the trace, a figure of divinity can manifest itself, but we now encounter only the trace of the trace as an indication of the gods' departure (HW, 250, 253, 272). To mark out what is salutary (*das Heile*) requires that one heed and re-trace the trace of the trace.

One evident reason for Heidegger's choice of Rilke's "improvised verses" is that the poem allows him to develop a sequence of "fundamental words," proceeding from "nature" to "the Open," which mirrors a sequence he follows in his meditation on Hölderlin's "As on a Feast Day . . ." (GA 4, 49–77). Heidegger thus seeks to situate Rilke with respect to the "poetizing thinking" initiated by Hölderlin. Whereas, for Hölderlin, "divinely beautiful nature" is the donation of the Open within which all that comes to presence enjoys its salutary "whiling" ("das Heil seiner Verweilung"; GA 4, 63), Rilke, on Heidegger's exegesis, understands "nature" metaphysically as self-willing will. Although he thinks nature, the "original ground of our Being," as a favoring releasement (*Mögen, Loswurf*), he does not think it in keeping with the early Greek experience of *physis*, namely, as an arising into un-concealment. Rather, according to Heidegger, the "original ground" becomes, for Rilke, transformed into the "unheard midst" ("die unerhörte Mitte"), the still center which, while exposing beings to the danger of their unprotected course, also keeps them gathered to itself by its steady pull and held secure within the serene balance of the "entire draw" ("der ganze Bezug"). The earthly figure of solid ground has thus become transformed into the figure of a play of forces (Heidegger briefly recalls Leibniz's *vis viva activa*; HW, 256); but since this play is thought as the counterplay of and hidden harmony between the centrifugal and the centripetal forces, the pull of the center reasserts itself, negating the radical temporality of manifestation which Hölderlin speaks of as a destinal "whiling." Rather than thinking the "wagering dare" (*das Wagnis*) as radical temporality, Rilke, Heidegger finds, thinks it, with an ambiguity characteristic of metaphysical reason, as both the wagering and daring midst and ground of beings, and as beings themselves which essentially are "what is wagered and dared as a whole." The Differing is thus effaced in that, as Heidegger concludes, in Rilke's poetic vocabulary, "the gravity of the pure forces, the unheard midst, the pure draw, the entire draw, the fullness of nature, life, and the wagering dare are the same" (HW, 261).

In keeping with this assimilation, Rilke does not think the Open as the clearing which allows beings to stand revealed in accordance with what Anaximander calls the *taxis* of time,[5] but rather as the intact sphere of the unimpeded draw, which, for Heidegger, is not the same as the Parmenidean sphere. The latter is rather the figure of Being's "unconcealing-lighting uniting," which does not constrain or totalize the realm of manifestation (HW, 278). Since Rilke supposedly thinks the Open as the unobstructed whole of all that is present or absent, that is, as completeness rather than as the clearing, he seeks to eliminate the obstructions and obscurations which are the work of representational, objectifying reason. He thus privileges non-rational "creation," the plants and animals that, caught up in the rapture of the "dull lust" which is their very act of being, dwell immediately within the Open.

The issue for Heidegger is not a theoretical refinement of thought but a transformative understanding of the afflictions and destitution which menace the age. Since he considers such affliction to have an essential or onto-historical character rather than to be a mere accident of history, he demands of poets and thinkers (and not, as might seem more natural, of political theorists and activists) a discerning engagement and vision capable of pointing out the way to a surmounting of danger. Danger is understood here as the sweeping totalization that, for Heidegger, is the hidden essence of technicity. The latter, he insists, consummates "the long-concealed essence of will which has long held sway as the Being of beings" (HW, 267). Will, in turn, is analyzed as having the character of unconditional command, as the self-assertion of the representational posit ("des vorsätzlichen Sichdurchsetzens"), which brings together, in undifferentiated unity, productive procurement and representational objectification (the English language cannot replicate the complex articulation of the posit as *stellen* and *setzen* in Heidegger's analysis). Modern science (in its character of reductive totalization) and totalitarian political organization are both, Heidegger concludes, the necessary consequences and "retinue" (*Gefolge*) of essential technicity. Notwithstanding the fact that Heidegger's essentializing of technicity (which allows him to dismiss, the year after Hiroshima, "the much discussed atom bomb"; HW, 271), together with his sweeping assimilation of metaphysical reason, technicity, and totalitarian politics, is itself a totalizing gesture, one must respect the fact that the focal concern of his agonized *Auseinandersetzung* with Rilke is the totalitarian temptation to which his own intellectual passions had rendered him susceptible. He now projects this temptation upon the organizing constraints of the Western intellectual tradition in its departure from pre-Socratic "experience."

The challenge Heidegger faces is to develop a thinking which exceeds the self-accomplishment of metaphysics and which is distinct from what he regards as Rilke's still intra-metaphysical critique of metaphysical reason. What renders this task particularly difficult is the evident close kinship between some of Rilke's and Heidegger's own important concerns, notably the relationship between authenticity and death and the exhortation to be attentive to the humble things of nature and of daily use, as contrasted with the casual attention given to mere commodities.[6] Do these focal concerns which Rilke shares with Heidegger not enable him to accomplish a "more originally formative overcoming" of the "imageless formations" (*bildlose Gebilde*) of technicity?[7]

Heidegger points out, first of all, that the issue in this preoccupation with things is not mere nostalgia for a vanishing ancestral way of life but the frame-up of what he will eventually call the "enframing" or "posure" (*Ge-stell*), which, in obstructing (*verstellen*) the Open, posits and "frames" (*stellt*) man himself as the functionary of technicity, and which unleashes rampant totalization (*totale Organisation*; HW, 272). Whatever Heidegger's personal leanings toward the traditional way of life of *Schwarzwald* peasantry, his attentiveness to "the thing" cannot be dismissed as an apolitical retreat.

With respect to Rilke, Heidegger's critical focus is trained on what Hamacher describes as "the master trope of Hegelian philosophy—negation of negation, speculative inversion," which, as "the consolidation of meaning and the universalizing of subjectivity," gives even to death and disintegration a positive import.[8]

The Rilkean inversion that springs from a resolve "to read the word 'death' without negativity"[9] relies, Heidegger finds, on a strategy of interiorization which outstrips calculative rationality and the immanence of consciousness (with its neglect of the image or aspect of things) in favor of "the inmost of the inner," the inner space of the heart. Although, for Rilke, this apotheosis of interiorization which outstrips consciousness or reason reverses the representational and production-oriented turn away from the Open, Heidegger concludes that the inner space of the world (*Weltinnenraum*) or the heart, made accessible by interiorizing remembrance (*Erinnerung*), shows itself, nevertheless, to be the sphere of subjectivity rather than the true Parmenidean sphere. It obscures the radical temporality of manifestation that constitutes "the original unity of that time-space as which Being itself holds sway" (HW, 283). Heidegger asserts:

> For Rilke's poetry, the Being of beings is determined metaphysically as worldly presence, which presence remains related to representational consciousness, whether the latter has the character of calculative representation or of the inward turning into the Open which is heartwardly accessible. (HW, 297)

One would expect the analysis to conclude here. Surprisingly, however, Heidegger carries it forward into hopeless ambiguity. Convinced that to be what Rilke calls "more daring still" than the wagering dare—if only "by a breath"—means to "dare it with language," he attempts to repeat Rilke's "basic words" as a different saying. This saying is to articulate not self-willing will but "the willingness of the more saying ones." In the end, Heidegger seeks to voice his own insights and his response to the destitution of the age in the poetic language he has exhaustively criticized, while also affirming the insurpassability of Hölderlin's poetic thought which reaches across and beyond destitution into the futurity of the pure advent.

To Dare It With Language

The ambiguity and irresolution just outlined derive, in part, from Heidegger's refusal—shared with much of the tradition of Rilke interpretation—to consider the divergence of *lexis* and interpretation in Rilke's poetic diction, or, in simpler terms, the non-coincidence of the saying with what is ostensibly being said. What he loses sight of, in the words of de Man, is the fact "that these [Rilke's] highly reflected statements directly implicate language as a category of meaning and thematize some of the lexicological and rhetorical aspects of poetic diction."[10]

Coming from Heidegger, such a refusal is surprising, for he seeks to rejoin the poet precisely as one of the "more daring ones" who will "dare it with language"; and he persistently dislocates the interlocution of poet and thinker from the philosophemes of subjectivity to the pure "speaking of language" ("das Sprechen der Sprache"). Given that, for Heidegger, language is emphatically not instrumental, ancillary, expressive, or deictic, his conviction that in its poetic articulation it remains, nevertheless (to echo de Man), "entirely truthful" can only be understood in terms of his rethinking of the very notion of truth. Since this rethinking of truth as the event of manifestation renders it strictly indissociable from the revelatory character of language, and since this revelatory function is thought, in both its lighting and concealing aspects, with reference to epochal historicity (thus diachronically rather than synchronically), Heidegger lacks access to the self-referential opacity and self-subversion of poetic language at the completion or closure of modernity. His privileging of diachronicity over synchronicity (which stands, of course, in sharp contrast to the opposite tendency in structuralism, which is part of the heritage of deconstruction) brings with it a certain disregard for *lexis* and structure in favor of the event-like singularity and the etymological historicality of the singularized word.

For Heidegger, then, it is language which bestows presencing or the opening for and the configurations of what becomes manifest. Language is essentially apophantic; but the two forms of essential untruth which menace all *apophansis* (concealment and obstruction or dissemblance)[11] nevertheless do not spring from language as such. Presumably, insofar as they are essential, they would still obtain should there be, *per impossibile*, another way to open up the space of the clearing. Heidegger's apophantic focus debars him from a poetry and poetics of sheer figuration that, quite apart from any revelatory function (even as trace or as pure expectancy of what is to come) thematizes both the self-containment and the radical insufficiency of poetic language, of the poem as figure articulating and disarticulating itself at the limits of silence. Such a poetry and poetics—neglected by Heidegger (together with its "groundwords," if not rather "flightwords" and "spacewords") is that of the late Rilke, notably in the *Sonnets to Orpheus* and in much of the work written after 1912. The articulations of the figure or of the dynamic trajectories which constitute it are focused here on non-closure:

> Alles ist weit—, und nirgends schliesst sich der Kreis.
> Sieh in der Schüssel, auf heiter bereitetem Tische,
> Seltsam der Fische Gesicht.
>
> Fische sind stumm . . . meinte man einmal. Wer weiss?
> Aber ist nicht am Ende ein Ort, wo man das, was der Fische
> Sprache wäre, *ohne* sie spricht?[12]

The smooth complementarity of "both halves" of the pseudo-Parmenidean sphere is ruptured here even at the humble level of eating. Although eater and eaten are intimately conjoined, their union cannot close the circle; in its approximation to, yet perpetual shortfall of, closure, it is characterized by what Merleau-Ponty (whose thought Rilke often anticipates) calls non-coincidence, the style of bodily reflection. Since the eaten are to be taken up into the very substance of the eater, they are not objects over against the latter, let alone a genuine Other; yet, unlike sheer *hylē*, on which the eater, on an Aristotelian analysis, would impress his *eidos*, the fish in the bowl have a vis-age (*Gesicht*) which enigmatically looks at the eater. Similarly, in Rilke's 1907 poem "Der Ball" ("The Ball," I.637f)—which he continued to regard as his most accomplished inscription of pure motion— the thrown projectile, from its high vantage point, suddenly choreographs the throwers "like a dance figure," revealing and assigning to them "a new place." As the spatiality of the thrown ball is indissociable from, yet non-coincident with, that of the thrower, so the time of the eater is interlinked but not synchronous with that of the eaten; and the language which would heal the latter's muteness can be spoken, at last, only "without them."

The "law" of the figure which interlinks eater and eaten, momentum and "home-weight" (*Heimgewicht*), flight and fall, is the law of their non-coincident reversibility. Unlike the Anaximandrian *taxis* of time, which conjoins arising and perishing without residue, allowing beings to "make recompense to one another" for the usurpation involved in their existence, the temporality of the Rilkean figure sustains polar opposites in the "gathering" of their unstilled tension. It resembles therein the "polemic" configuration of the Heraclitean "tropics of fire" (*pyros tropai*; Fr. 31), which set in motion a *perpetuum mobile* of non-totalizable referrals and reversals that subvert the apparent pure self-identity of the polarized opposites. These subverting reversals articulate themselves as the very tropology of the Heraclitean *logos*, as figure.

Figuration, as the chiasmatic (hence non-coincident) interconnection of seemingly dissevered polarities, is not fully achieved in natural or created "plastic" form—not even in the fountain or cascade which Rilke favored as the accomplished reconciliation of form and flux. It is achieved, rather, through the "inward-turning" of the tropology of a poetic language which articulates itself, at the limits of the sayable, as "ingathered throw" (*gesammelter Wurf*). As de Man emphasizes,[13] Rilke's "inner space of the world," created, in part, through the interiorizing labor of remembrance (*Erinnerung*), is not the metaphysical domain of subjective interiority (as Heidegger construes it), but a realm of poetic figuration freed from the referentiality of ordinary language or from what Rilke himself calls "the languages of man": communication, conceptualization, and poetic symbolization.[14] To dare it with language becomes, for Rilke, to approximate an absolute language no longer subservient to the constraints of comprehension and communication. Commenting on his acute experience of the failure of any received poetic language when he was faced, during his travels in Spain in 1912–13, with the grandeur and "extremity" of the Spanish landscapes, Rilke writes:

Appearance and vision came together everywhere—in the object, as it were—in every thing a whole inner world was put forward, as if an angel, encompassing space, were blind and gazed into himself. This world, no longer contemplated from a human vantage point, but in the angel, constitutes, perhaps, my true calling.[15]

The world contemplated within the angel already possesses "the unheard, insurpassable intensity of the inner equivalents"; that is, it articulates itself as a pure, heightened, agitated, surpassing poetic diction. This diction, as intuitable (*anschaulich*), accomplishes the quasi-visible presencing of what Merleau-Ponty calls the invisible of the visible, given in the visible. It is "inner" without ceasing to be world; in being raised beyond human meaning, it rejoins, in the words of Merleau-Ponty (who refers here to Valéry), "the very voice of the things, the waves, and the forests."[16] Earthly things are thus not deprived of their "gravity" or density but are transmuted into ciphers of a "positive silence" that does not simply recapture and restore a silence which is pre-linguistic.

Remarking on the paradox that, whereas the *Duino Elegies* "advocate a conception of language that excludes all subjective and intersubjective dimensions," affirming instead "the primacy of the signifier," they nevertheless seek to engage the reader at the level of pathos, de Man notes that a poetic language freed of all referential constraints remains strictly inconceivable.[17] Rilke's absolute poetic language, the "language of angels," or even "of the gods," however, is not a Mallarméan pure formalism or a sheer play of signifiers; it results, rather, from a process of cosmic "sedimentation" (*Niederschlag*) and alchemical trans-substantiation, which refines and sublates rather than eliminates the gross and the ordinary. For this reason, Rilke can say in the *Sonnets* that we truly *live* only in figures ("denn wir leben wahrhaft in Figuren"; I, 738).

The language of pure figuration corresponds to what "would be" the language of beings in their silence, spoken "without them," not by the eater and user but by angels or gods, as what Wodtke calls "their mute, uninterpretable gesture."[18] To achieve such an "earthly correspondence" (*irdische Entsprechung*), poetic language must dare to situate itself in the chiasm, at the precarious intersection of two silences, of which one is pre-linguistic and the other in excess of language. Faithful as it is to the "gravity" of things in their silence, poetic figuration retains an opacity that renders it—for all its intensity and exaltation—incapable of the essential-historical vision which Heidegger finds in Hölderlin and prizes as a response to the deflections of need in a destitute time.

The Empty Midst

Language at its most extreme daring is, for Rilke, poetic figuration, which, like the "dance-figure" accomplished by the young woman to whose memory he dedicated the *Sonnets*, momentarily achieves the ungrounded, dynamic stability of accomplished form gathered out of transience:

> . . . Du, fast noch Kind, ergänze
> für einen Augenblick die Tanzfigur
> zum reinen Sternbild eines jener Tänze
> darin wir die dumpf ordnende Natur
>
> vergänglich übertreffen . . .[19]

With their striking parallels of thought and diction to the "improvised verses" cited by Heidegger, these lines show that the "greater daring" by which we surpass "nature's dull order" is not subjective interiority but artistic configuration, which hearkens back to the "unheard midst," the place where "the lyre / rose sonorously" in the time of Orpheus, briefly enabling even vegetal and bestial nature to become "fully hearing." The young dancer, mindful of this place, is literally "moved" (and "slightly estranged" from the present order of things) by her bond to the archaic time "when Orpheus sang."

De Man, noting that Rilke privileges the phonic over the semantic function of language, concludes that the metaphor of the musical instrument "does not represent for him the subjectivity of a consciousness, but a potential inherent in language."[20] However, such a privileging of the phonic materiality of language over its semantic aspects still amounts to no more than the sort of intra-metaphysical rebellion against metaphysical hierarchies that Heidegger criticizes; it turns the tables without challenging the structure. In German poetry, such a challenge fully asserts itself only with Celan's dismemberments and reconfigurations of a language which was not unambiguously his own and whose semantic energies he released, disseminated, and subverted.

Rather than attribute to Rilke an "absolute phonocentrism" (as does de Man, in particular with respect to *The Book of Hours*),[21] however, one needs to remember that the place where the poet's lyre resounds, the enabling center of the figure, which, as the "gravitational point," is the nexus of all its lines of force, is for him the empty and "unheard" midst. Without attention to the silent blankness, withdrawn from both light and *phonē*, of this dynamic space of emptiness, the tensional balance of the figure cannot be achieved.

Although Rilke's empty and nameless midst is clearly more than the void space necessary for maneuverability, the negativity allowing for inversion, as de Man describes it,[22] and certainly is more or other than the pure self-willing will of Heidegger's interpretation, this excess only bespeaks itself in some of Rilke's last poems. Even in the *Sonnets to Orpheus*, the midst is still often subservient to the metaphysical trope of reversal:

> jener entwerfende Geist, welcher das Irdische meistert,
> liebt in dem Schwung der Figur nichts wie den wendenden Punkt.[23]

From spirit to "project," mastery, and reversal or inversion, the metaphysical schema announces itself here.

In Rilke's "shawl poems" of 1923, however—a series inspired by a collection of Kashmiri shawls in the historical museum at Berne—the midst is articulated differently:

> . . .während du sie siehst, die leichthin ausgesparte
> Mitte des Kashmirshawls, die aus dem Blumenraum
> sich schwarz erneut und klärt aus ihres Rahmens Kante
> und einen reinen Raum schafft für den Raum . . .:
> erfährst du dies: das Namen sich an ihr
> endlos verschwenden: denn sie ist die Mitte.
> Wie es auch sei, das Muster unsrer Schritte,
> um eine solche Leere wandeln wir.[24]

The nameless midst in its blankness and ease is here not the pivot enabling reversal; rather, it ceaselessly renews and clarifies itself in and through the figured space which it opens up, the "space of flowers." Its very blankness, which seemed, at first, subservient to the figure becomes the focus, whereas the figure, being relegated to the border, retreats into marginality. Nevertheless, without the figured border, the empty midst could not hold out to the viewer the possibility of dwelling in its own black clarity.

Rilke, however, only rarely responds positively to such an invitation of dwelling in emptiness. Rather, the midst often appears treacherous; for, although it is indispensable to the figure's dynamic repose, it seems also to mark the failure of figuration, its lie. When Rilke has to acknowledge that the figure fails on account of the emptiness at its core, its lack of substantiality or inherent reality, that even the "stellar interrelation" deceives, his move is usually to affirm with proud but tragic resignation that the self-sufficient perfection of poetic form is, after all, temporal:

> Doch uns freue eine Weile nun
> der Figur zu glauben. Das genügt.[25]

The totalizing reversal which converts negativity into spiritual gain is here not really abandoned as delusory; it is merely renounced as unachievable. In the end, Rilke's renunciation of closure and ultimate meaning in favor of sheer poetic figuration remains close to despair, leaving every long insatisfaction still crying in the heart.

At its deepest level, Heidegger's interlocution with Rilke concerns the thought of the empty opening, which is Heidegger's own sustained concern. In "The Origin of the Work of Art," Heidegger already speaks of the opening or clearing in strikingly Rilkean language:

> In the midst of beings as a whole, there essentially is an open place. There is a clearing. Thought of in terms of beings, it has more Being than beings. This open midst, therefore, is not enclosed by beings; but all beings, rather, encircle the lighting midst itself, like the nothing, which we scarcely know. (HW, 41)

In "What Are Poets For?", Heidegger insists on thinking the Parmenidean sphere with respect to the "unconcealing midst" that releases all presencing and repudiates totalization. The task, for Heidegger, is not only to demarcate this sphere with its "unshaken heart,"[26] against the throw and counterthrow, the perpetual disequilibrium, of the Rilkean ball, and against the polarities and reversals of the "sphere of subjectivity," but also to gain, through interlocution with the poets, another vantage point for history and action. As Heidegger stresses in the first "Preliminary Remark" of his 1959 lecture, "Hölderlins Erde und Himmel" ("Hölderlin's Earth and Sky"), the issue is whether, in our present historical epoch (*Weltalter*), we are able "to belong to Hölderlin's poetry." The thinking which seeks such a belonging is described as

> . . . an attempt to transmute (*umstimmen*) our habitual [mode of] representation into a non-habitual, because simple, thinking experience. (The transmutation into the thinking experience of the midst of the infinite relation—: out of the posure (*Ge-stell*) as the self-dissimulating coming-into-its-own (*Ereignis*) of the Fourfold.) (GA 4, 133)

Only from the vantage point of the empty midst can the thinker who follows the poet speak—without prescription—to an age which "hangs in the abyss."

Heidegger's Parmenidean sphere remains, nevertheless, a figure of completeness, cohesion, and centered equipoise. The song of the poets who are the "more daring ones" celebrates, he concludes, "the inviolateness of the sphere of Being" (HW, 294). Heidegger's effort to rethink Western intellectual history remains an effort to complete the circle or sphere by joining end to beginning (in disregard of Alkmaion's saying that men are mortals precisely insofar as they cannot do so [Fr.2]). Although he insists that "the spherical does not rest in a circumference which comprises, but in the unconcealing midst which, lighting, shelters what presences" (HW, 278), his rhetoric tends to lag behind the extreme labor of his thinking, affecting the latter with its predilections. One suspects that his problematic critique of Rilke is a struggle against certain limitations of his own rhetoric. Given Heidegger's charge that Rilke thinks the sphere only "with regard to beings in the sense of the completeness of all of its sides" and that, therefore, the Open is, for him, ultimately "the closed" of the unrestricted interaction of the "pure forces," it is instructive to consider what is perhaps Rilke's most daring and realized articulation of the Open as the empty midst. I cite here in its entirety one of his last poems, "Mausoleum," dating from October 1924:

> Königsherz. Kern eines hohen
> Herrschertums. Balsamfrucht.
> Goldene Herznuss. Urnen-Mohn
> mitten im Mittelbau,
> (wo der Widerhall abspringt,
> wie ein Splinter der Stille,
> wenn du dich rührst,
> weil es dir scheint,
> dass deine vorige
> Haltung zu laut war . . .)
> Völkern entzogenes,
> sterngesinnt,
> in unsichtbaren Kreisen
> kreisendes Königsherz.
>
> Wo ist, wohin,
> jenes der leichten
> Lieblingin?
> :Lächeln, von aussen,
> auf die zögernde Rundung
> heiterer Früchte gelegt;
> oder der Motte vielleicht,
> Kostbarkeit, Florflügel, Fühler . . .
>
> Wo aber, wo, das sie sang,
> das sie in Eins sang,
> das Dichterherz?
> :Wind,
> unsichtbar,
> Windinnres.[27]

The kingly heart of the pharaoh, the seat of one who was the soul of a people, has withdrawn into inwardness. Withdrawn for millennia into "the midst of the middle structure," it has become the "poppy of urns," increasingly oblivious to all earthly clamor and attachments. In its renunciation and repose, it is mindful of the emptiness at the heart of figuration.

The heart of the beloved, by contrast, had divested itself of inwardness, expending itself lightly upon the world. Like a smile, it has bestowed itself "from without" upon the most transient of earthly things, the gaily ripening fruit and the wingdust of moths, thus consummating its own realization of the emptiness of the subject or self. Indeed, whereas for metaphysical reason subjective interiority is at the enabling center of manifestation, the beloved's heart-dispersal, her relinquishment of interiority, is at the very center and core of Rilke's poem. It displaces the sort of interiorization that, according to Heidegger, "only commutes insistingly (*durch-setzend*) willing *essence* (*Wesen*) into the inmost invisible of the heart's space" (HW, 285).

The poet's heart, lastly, "sang into one" the king's lofty inwardness and the queen's loving heart-bestowal, uniting the inner with the outer emptiness by a conjugal bond. This union is not a totalizing closure, for it is accomplished by one whose own heart is empty, being "wind" or "wind's inner." The mausoleum that enshrines in its midst the "heartnut" and "kernel" has here become a wind-crypt; it assigns the clear space of emptiness to any possible interlocution between poetry and thinking.

For both Heidegger and Rilke, it is ultimately language that builds this wind-crypt, whether it be thought of as *Gespräch* or as pure poetic figuration. One may recall here Gerald L. Bruns's comment that, for Heidegger,

> poetry now has to be understood in terms of renunciation (*Verzicht*) of linguistic mastery. This means understanding poetry as the *Sichversagen* of the poet where poetry opens itself—enters into, listens, or belongs to—the mystery of language, its otherness, its non-humanness, its density, its danger.[28]

Only in the wind-crypt of figuration can Heidegger and Rilke, at the extreme of their daring (which reaches beyond either tragic rhetoric or eschatological vision), be said or sung into one. Poetic language can at least initiate, though probably not consummate, the realization that Heidegger strives for in his interlocution with the poets: the realization of the empty midst that is the "unshaken heart" of manifestation. Heidegger, indeed, holds that such interlocution (*Gespräch*) can accomplish what poetic language alone tends to fall short of; he insists, however, that there can be no realization which surpasses language.

4

◆

Textuality and the Question of Origin: Heidegger's Reading of 'Andenken' and 'Der Ister'

Mais l'*un* du sens n'advient pas. Ce n'est pas
qu'il n'y ait pas de sens. Mais l'inavènement de
l'un du sens est cela seul qui compte dans le
sens. Que cette chose unique survive dans le
sens au sens! "Hölderlin," pour nous, est le
nom de cette survivance ...

> Jean-Luc Nancy, "La Joie d'Hypérion"

But the one *of meaning does not arrive. Not*
that there is no meaning. But the non-advent of
the unity of meaning is what alone counts with
respect to meaning. May this unique thing
survive within meaning unto meaning!
"Hölderlin," for us, is the name of this
survival ...

"Is there a text in itself?" Heidegger asks, in concluding a letter to Detlev Lüders, who had expressed his puzzlement as to how a text "re-examined in accordance with the original drafts" could be said to "rest upon" an attempt at interpretation. Although Heidegger declares himself willing to strike his "impossible remark" concerning the priority of interpretation, he rejects as "trivial" any simple-minded insistence on the primacy of the critically established text. His repudiation suggests not so much an awareness that

44

such texts (and certainly the texts of Hölderlin as well as those of Presocratic philosophy) are themselves products of interpretation, as his own interpretive preoccupation with the *essential* "unsaid." It is the latter which determines for him *"when* [a text] is fully appropriated as a text"—a question which, in its turn, cannot be divorced from "the *essential* Being of language and of linguistic tradition."[1] In the end, instead of striking the offending statement, he is content to modify it with textual devices such as underlinings and quotation marks.

What is a text? The question becomes particularly unsettling when, as in Heidegger's "annotations" to or "elucidations" of Hölderlin's poetry (or of other poets whom he situates in Hölderlin's *Wirkungsgeschichte*), the text becomes the unassignable meeting ground of an interlocution or *Zwie-sprache* that expropriates both poet and thinker. This expropriation derives not only from Heidegger's often (and irritatingly) expressed contempt for literary scholarship and for the entire "enterprise" of literature (so that the poet is cast as the thinker's precursor), but also from his admitted recourse to the supplement (*Beigabe*). As he remarks at the outset of his 1942 lecture course on Hölderlin's fragmentary hymn "Der Ister," his selection of poems to be discussed is guided by the envisaged "annotations," which themselves function in the capacity of supplement. Therefore, he remarks:

> It may be that much, or even everything, which is thus annotated is, to be sure, superadded and does not "stand in" the poetry. The annotations are then not taken from the poetry but are presented (*vorgelegt*) from out of it . . . These annotations provide, at the risk of missing the truth of Hölderlin's poetry, only certain memorial marks (*Merk-male*), signs to provoke attentiveness (*für das Aufmerken*), footholds for thoughtful consideration.[2]

He concludes these remarks with the rather puzzling admission that, nevertheless, the poetry itself must always be "what is first and present"; it must, in the end, legitimate the interpretation which had offered to it a procrustean bed.

The question of the text gains urgency with respect to Heidegger's reading of Hölderlin, owing to several considerations. The poetic text is, first of all, an art-work; and, as Annemarie Gethmann-Siefert notes, it is one of the "neuralgic points" of Heidegger's reading of poetry that he "hypostatizes" the art-work (by rendering it *essentially* independent of human activity and culture), allowing it to become "the interpretive horizon for human destiny."[3] Where and how, in the interlocution between poet and thinker, does the poetic text as art-work configure itself?

Second, Heidegger's studies of Hölderlin function in the context of a self-proclaimed displaced and encrypted "confrontation" (*Auseinanderset-zung*) with the ideology and politics of National Socialism (which, in

Heidegger's view, had betrayed its promise or "its inner truth and great-ness"), and thus with the logic, mythology, and rhetoric of totalization (which itself involved an appropriation of Hölderlin).[4] As concerns the text, Rodolphe Gasché suggests that the very gesture of interpretive "elucida-tion" is inherently totalizing, since it rests upon "an operation of decision-making in a totalizing perspective."[5] Heidegger seems implicitly to ac-knowledge as much when he speaks, in curiously metaphysical idiom, of the text as resting on its interpretation, which constitutes a posited ground ("ist zugrunde gelegt").[6] A "literary" reading, according to Gasché, can resist the totalizing tendency of interpretation by eroding textual propriety as a basis for interpretive decisions:

> *reading* is the reading of the text's unreadability, that is, of its structural incapacity to lend itself to univocal and unproblematic totalization.[7]

Despite Heidegger's expropriation of poet and thinker, and his displace-ment of them into the straits of interlocution, his insistence on the *essential* unsaid as the unitary source of textual configuration repudiates unreadabil-ity, the antidote to totalization. The situation is similar with respect to Heidegger's reading of non-poetic texts, notably those of Greek philosophy.

Finally, the question of the text obtrudes itself when—as in Heidegger's meditations on "Andenken" and "Der Ister" to be here considered—the issue in the *Zwiesprache* between poet and thinker is *oriri*, the origin, as to its position, its relation to history, its singularity, its differential character, and the possibility of its commemorative retrieval. What is the relation of the text, as Heidegger understands it, and of its "memorial" constitution (through the supplementary *Merk-male*) to the position of origin and to the issue of commemoration?

These questions will be pursued here along three lines of approach, with a focus on Heidegger's lecture courses "Andenken" and "Der Ister" (which are closely related in time and themes), together with his subsequent essay "Andenken" (GA 4, 79–151). The first strand of questioning will address the *essential*-political concerns that, in displacement, constrain Heidegger's reading of the two hymns, and the character of his encrypted "confronta-tion" with totalitarian politics. From this vantage point, it will be possible to consider the relationship between a philosophical critique of totalization and the totalizing tendencies of interpretation. The second strand will solicit the interpretive moves of Heidegger's reading and its tensional relationship to Hölderlin's poetic articulation, which is to say, the reconfiguration of the text. Of special concern here will be the function of the supplement. The third strand, finally, will address the issue of the origin of the text as art-work in relation to the problematic of origin, and consider whether the intertext configured in the interlocution of poet and thinker allows for a reading which the interlocutors no longer govern.

I

Heidegger's guiding concern, in his reading of the two Hölderlinian hymns, is with the destinal mandate of Germania (which becomes, for him, the mythically idealized figure of Germany) in the context of Occidental, and ultimately planetary, destiny. In his understanding of Germania and of her destinal role, *essential* and *historico-political* thought-structures are ambiguously conflated. Germany's privilege, its election at a particular historical moment (to speak with bitter irony, since the moment was that of the Shoah), is its guardianship of the Differing, which supposedly accrues to it through its kinship to ancient Greece. This kinship rests upon what Heidegger considers to be a sameness of linguistic and poetic traditions; the German people, in his view, are now "the people of poets and thinkers."[8] This conviction accounts for the fact that the greater part of Heidegger's lecture course on the Ister hymn is devoted to Sophocles and to Greek thought in general; and it underlies the philosopher's repeated and astonishing diatribes against techno-Anglo-Americanization, of which the following excerpt can serve as an illustration:

> We know today that the Anglo-Saxon world of Americanism is determined to annihilate Europe, which is to say, its homeland and the beginning of the Occidental . . . The entry of America into this planetary war is not an entry into history, but is already the final American act of American ahistoricity and self-devastation . . . The concealed spirit of the originary in the Occident will not even reserve for this process of the self-devastation of what is devoid of a beginning the glance of contempt, but will await, out of the releasement (*Gelassenheit*) of the repose of the originary, its stellar hour. (GA 53, 68)

Of particular concern for Heidegger, in this context, is the Anglo-Americanization of language, which he fears may govern even the study and translation of ancient Greek. It is therefore of the greatest importance, he holds, to consider carefully not only what foreign languages one chooses to learn but also in what spirit one acquires the foreign language of choice, which is ancient Greek:

> We learn the Greek language so that the concealed *essence* of our own historical beginning may, for us, find its way into the clarity of our word . . . We may learn the Greek language only if we must learn it, due to *essential* historical necessity, out of our own German language. (GA 53, 81)

These thought-structures may, in general, be characterized as the form of Heidegger's interpretation of the Hölderlinian figure of the "patriotic turning," as interlinking Germany and the Occident with "Oriental" Greece.

For Hölderlin, as Allemann has convincingly argued,[9] the "patriotic turning" (*vaterländische Umkehr*) primarily interlinks the earthly realm, governed by the "kingly" principle of law and measure, with the fiery death-world, the realm of the withdrawing gods, which is characterized by the Empedoclean principle of "eccentric enthusiasm." Since Hölderlin considers the passionate excess or "madness" of the fiery realm to be the natal element of the Greek spirit (in contrast to Heidegger's ponderously reflective portrayal of the Greeks), while that of the Occidental spirit is formal clarity or lucid articulation, the patriotic turning marks also the proper relationship between Greece and Hesperia. Sterility or destruction threatens a people or culture that closes itself off to what is alien to it or refuses the homeward turn out of formative exile. Thus Hölderlin, in the hymnic fragment " . . . Meinest du es solle gehen . . .," ascribes the perishing of ancient Greece to what might be called its Apollonian infatuation, which induced it to neglect its natal element:

> . . . Nemlich sie wollten stiften
> Ein Reich der Kunst. Dabei ward aber
> Das Vaterländische von ihnen
> Versäumet und erbärmlich gieng
> Das Griechenland, das schönste, zu Grunde.[10]

Heidegger understands the patriotic turning as, first of all, the coming-into-its-own of a privileged form of historical human existence, that of Germany, which has an *essential* relationship to the Greek-Oriental fire. Through this relationship (founded on poetic articulation), it has exposed itself to the enigma of the origin, which must now be mindfully recollected and given articulation (within the element of northern clarity), so as to make possible a human dwelling upon the earth. Such a mode of dwelling is able to resist the growing rootlessness and the reduction of all presencing to mere resource at one's disposal (*Bestand*), which Heidegger ascribes to technicity. The patriotic turning is then "patriotic" also in the sense that it restores mortals to the earth as their homeland or *patria*, which is here demarcated—not against the Hölderlinian fire nor even against "world" as understood in "The Origin of the Work of Art"[11]—but over against the reign of *Bestand* as rampant totalization. Heidegger's "confrontation" with National Socialism centers on the point that, as he remarks in the *Der Spiegel* interview, it "did indeed go in this direction" of seeking to attain a proper relationship to the *essence* of technicity but proved "too poorly equipped for thought" to achieve the requisite historical understanding.[12]

Heidegger interprets the quasi-dialectical relationship between the natal and the alien as an espousal of the alien and unhomelike (*des Unheimischen*), for the sake of becoming at-home in "one's own," which is one's mortal situation. The alien, understood in this sense, is that which always-was (*das Gewesene*), the enigma to which early Greek thinking and poetizing was exposed. An *essential* understanding of the alien and the natal (as *das Gewesene* in contrast to particular world-configurations) is here ambiguously conflated with an historically and geographically concretized understanding (as Germany's relation to ancient Greece). The figure of the Ister, the "stream of the homeland" (the Danube), which, as Heidegger notes, flows hesitantly and darkly near its source, as if affected by the countersurge of the distant sea, and which bears for Hölderlin the "alien name" that the Romans gave to its lower course, serves as the figure of the patriotic turning in the double and conflated senses.

For Heidegger, the highest achievement of the Greek spirit, insofar as it accomplished the homeward turning, was the founding of the *polis* and thus the instauration of the political, which Heidegger insists on understanding out of the aletheic character of the *polis*:

> Only by passing through what is alien to them, [through] the ability for cool self-containment, does their own become their property. Out of the severity of a poetizing, thinking, form-giving containment alone are they able to encounter the gods in lucidly articulated presence. This is their founding and building of the *polis* as the *essential* site of history which is determined by the holy. The *polis* determines the political. (GA 4, 87f)

Heidegger develops this thought further in his lecture course on Parmenides, offered in the winter term of 1942/43, immediately following the Ister-hymn lectures.[13] He there develops an understanding of the *polis* as the gathering "pole" of manifestation, which depends for its salutary rather than "tragic" configuration on aletheic measure. The "death-gravid passage" of mortals, which circles from the *polis* to what Heidegger calls, in the language of the concluding myth of Plato's *Republic*, *to tēs lēthēs pedion*, "oblivion's field," requires them to partake of the waters of Lethe (GA 54, 175–182). As long as Lethe enters the aletheic domain of the *polis* in proper measure, functioning as the donation of "the uncanny," it calls forth Mnemosyne, the mother of the Muses, and thus "the *essential inception* of poesy" (GA 54, 133f). Aletheic measure here takes the place of the proper balance between the kingly and Empedoclean principles. Its establishment is the task of the "spirit of the stream" (*Stromgeist*), which, as "poetic spirit," is what Heidegger calls "the wandering of the becoming-at-home of historical man upon this earth" (GA 53, 37f). As such, it calls forth Mnemosyne to found and sustain a poetic dwelling upon the earth.

Gethmann-Siefert points out that Heidegger returns "to a manner of questioning constitutive of German Idealism," namely, to the ideal of unifying poetry and politics, as developed by Hegel and Hölderlin on the basis of Schiller's conception of the aesthetic education of man. She notes, however, that whereas Hegel, as well as Hölderlin, insisted on marking the interval between the Greek *polis* and contemporary historico-political configuration, Heidegger conflates it, together with the difference between political engagement and "the fictional character of interpretive performance."[14] Furthermore, she perceptively points out that:

> In Heidegger's philosophical interpretation of the poets, a critique of the foundational identification of the aesthetics of enlightenment decisive for early Idealism is lost: namely the rejection of the structural identification of the artist and statesman in the concept of genius, or rather . . . the conception of the "great individual."[15]

In virtue of these complex conflations, poetic instauration and the *essential* interlocution between poet and thinker become, for Heidegger, the decisive character of historico-political engagement and lend themselves, with their veneer of culture, beauty, and sophistication, to the legitimation of totalitarian politics.

Given his conflations, Heidegger does not hesitate to install his *essential* analysis at a concrete historico-political juncture, which he takes to be indicated by the "now" that is the emphatic first word of Hölderlin's Ister-hymn. This *kairos* functions for Heidegger in a manner similar to the vernal equinox in "Andenken": it conjoins decline (*Untergang*) and transition (*Übergang*) and calls for a "knowing readiness for one's belonging into destiny" (GA 4, 87). It is at such a historical juncture that the thinker must mediate, to a people supposedly gifted with a destinal mandate, the "word" of the poet.

Heidegger's reading of Hölderlin totalizes the text not only in Gasché's sense, namely, in that it legitimates a certain unitary (as well as historically prescriptive) reading, but also by its sweeping unification of Greece and Hesperia, antiquity and modernity, poetry and politics, interpretation and political action.

What ultimately enables Heidegger to reconcile these totalizing moves with his own insistence on differential articulation and on the thought of the Differing is a guiding distinction between spiritual and technical modalities of unification. This distinction becomes thematic, above all, in his discussions of the politics of the German university and thus of the institutionalization of knowledge. Heidegger, in this context, both deplored the increasing fragmentation and specialization of the intellectual disciplines (*Wissenschaften*) and also opposed the National Socialist ideal of "politicized science" (*staatliche Wissenschaft*), in favor of an *essentially* and "spiritually" based mode of unification. In the framework of his lecture courses on Hölderlin, his conviction that spiritual unification is inherently differential or "polemic," and thus non-totalizing, accounts for his blindness to his own tendency to totalize the Hölderlinian texts. It also makes for a persistent reference to and rhetoric of *Geist*, which cannot be explained merely through Hölderlin's poetic usage. Derrida, in particular, has called attention to the political import of this rhetoric.[16]

II

Heidegger's supplementation of Hölderlin's poetry not only dissembles (in keeping with the Derridean logic of the supplement) its own essential function behind an appearance of marginality (adding "annotations" to the text), but it also operates through the very act of *essentializing*. His readings select and gather (to echo his own play on three senses of *lesen*) the poetic texts out of the archipelago of their fragmentation and dispersion, in a manner which involves both a transposition into onto-history and at least a partial occlusion of finitude. Christopher Fynsk, in an insightful study of poetic finitude, characterizes this occlusion as follows:

> Hölderlin, however, did not, in the end, define a history by situating himself in relation to this promise [of saving amidst danger]. No doubt he tries, at times, to think this relationship in terms of an eschatology, thus projecting an end to that experience of a lack of measure which constantly demarcates itself in his efforts to establish an historical site for the advent of the holy. But to literalize this project, as does Heidegger . . . is to refuse to acknowledge that it takes form in a questioning which never closes, even during the time of his "madness."[17]

Heidegger's essentializing supplementation affects not only his readings of poetry (Hölderlin's and Trakl's, in particular) but also his reading of Sophocles and, in general, of the thought-structure of Greek tragedy from an Hölderlinian perspective, as articulated in the Ister-hymn lectures. In focusing on Heidegger's re-configuration of Hölderlin's hymns, the present study will, in the main, bypass this reading of Sophocles and will concern itself with the philosopher's interpretation of certain Hölderlinian tropes, notably those of greeting, of interconnection and mediation, and of a poetic founding of that which abides.

Every poetic word, for Heidegger, is "a greeting word" (GA, 4, 101), and this characterization carries a double sense. First, in the *essential* sense, greeting bespeaks mindfulness of the differential origin of manifestation; it holds in memory (*Andenken*) the enigma of the Differing as that which already-was (*das Gewesene*). In contrast to conceptual grasping, the gesture of greeting releases that which presences to show itself in its *essential* "whiling." At the same time, however, greeting opens up the historical place-scape of *essential* poetic practice. In coming-into-its-own (that is, into Germanic clarity), such poetizing keeps in memory the "alien" which it has sought out but surpassed, the Greek "fire from heaven." The poet therefore releases the wind to "go and greet" the fiery southern regions, while he himself remains behind, affirming his natal ground. Heidegger insists, furthermore, that what is greeted in such poetic commemoration "swings across" the straits of the present and encounters a people from out of the future, as what is still "to come." In greeting it, the poet and thinker prepare for its advent.

Heidegger thus fastens the complex articulation of his onto-historical vision (which involves the retrieval, in difference, of ancient Greece) onto the slight support of the poet's trope of greeting, and onto the identification of greeting with commemorating (*andenken*). Since commemoration involves partedness, Heidegger here *essentializes* (in a manner analogous to his reading of Trakl's *Abgeschiedenheit*) Hölderlin's thought of parting, which is poignantly articulated not only in the poem itself but in the two approximately contemporaneous letters to Böhlendorff that Heidegger cites.[18] Not only does he disregard the ontic aspects of partedness (from "days of love" and from the companionship of heroic labor) but he also reinterprets the articulation of parting on the level of the poet's diction. Partedness here bespeaks itself, in particular, through Hölderlin's insistent repetition of the qualifying and distancing *aber* (but), in which Heidegger perceives a stair-like progression and "fugue" of a "wandering coming-to-be-at-home in the ownmost." This wandering is not errant but shows the structure of the dialectical process of *Aufhebung*: every step is surpassed "in favor of the next one, yet without forgetting the one left behind" (GA 4, 151). Given that this wandering is commemoration (*andenken*) and greeting, the latter reveals itself as the preserving moment of an *Aufhebung* that, in Heidegger's understanding, no longer functions within a metaphysical economy.

Greeting, understood in this sense, constitutes an achievement of reconciliation or "destinal balance"; Heidegger thus speaks of it as "the eventuation (*Ereignis*) of festivity," of the bridal feast of divinities and mortals (GA 4, 105). Destinal balance is attained when these two come to encounter one another "out of their *essential* ground" (GA 52, 77). The fruit of their encounter, for Heidegger, is the poet thought of, on the model of the story of the birth of Eros in Plato's *Symposium*, as a mediating *daimōn* or "demi-god." However, whereas Platonic *erōs* empowers the individual to follow a path (likewise a stair-like progression) of intellectual and spiritual development, the poet's mediation accomplishes the historical instauration of a communal form of human existence (*Menschentum*), in the manner of the ungrounded grounding and the donation out of excess that Heidegger, in "The Origin of the Work of Art," identifies as modalities of a poetic founding of truth. The birth of the poet from out of the bridal feast is thus always also a historical beginning. Heidegger does not hesitate to point out, however, that the history at issue is "that of the Germans" (GA 4, 106); and he is still more explicit in his lectures on the Ister hymn, suggesting that the Germans might come to surpass the Greeks and their temples by learning to make their home in the alien (Greek) element of the heavenly fire (GA 53, 155). Hölderlin's poetry alone, he finds, articulates what requires to be poetized: the coming to be-at-home (*Heimisch-werden*) of the German *Menschentum* within Occidental history, as well as the distress (*Not*) of their current self-alienation (GA 53, 154f).

Heidegger's nationalistic vision, however, is essentialized and spiritualized: coming-to-be-at-home, as a modality of poetic dwelling, is understood as an orientation toward "the Open of the in-between" (GA 4, 148), where "the holy" can come to word and festively establish (*festigen*) itself. The Open is the empty "hearth" of human dwelling, poetized in "sameness" by Sophocles and Hölderlin, in keeping with the exigencies of their respective historical situations (GA 53, 153). In that the task of the poet is to poetize the "dwelling" of an historical form of human existence, from out of the quasi-dialectic between the homelike and the unhomelike, Heidegger likens "poetic spirit" to the "spirit of the stream" as poetized in Hölderlin's stream hymns; for it is the stream which unifies wandering (*Wanderschaft*) and localization (*Ortschaft*):

> The spirit of the stream is the poetic spirit which experiences the itineracy of being-in-the-unhomelike, and which "recollects" (*denkt an*, [in quotation marks]) the locality of coming-to-be-at-home. (GA 53, 175)

To the question, "What (Who?) is spirit?", which Heidegger asks pointedly in the Ister-hymn lectures,[19] he answers that it is what poetically enables historical forms of human dwelling to be upon the earth, by unifying the own and the alien, source and sea, origin and fulfillment. The poet, in founding a historical locality of human dwelling as a being-at-home of spirit, opens up a time-space for the appearance of "the holy" (GA 4, 114).

Heidegger is willing, of course, to acknowledge that Germany has not (as yet) realized its destinal mandate, which must be defined in relation to ancient Greece, and that its situation is one of "night" rather than of festivity. Night, however, is for him a figure of transition rather than of occlusion; it is a time marked by the expectancy of a new dawn. For this reason, he gives prominence, in his reading of "Andenken," not only to the vernal equinox but also to the linking "slow footbridges" (*langsame Stege*), and notes that greeting finds its fulfillment in the passage of the "cradling breezes" that drift across them, heavy with "golden dreams." Dreams are then interpreted as the figure of the incursion of the enigma of manifestation, whereas "gold" and "cradling" point back to the poet's birth out of the heavenly fire (GA 4, 111–116).

What is striking in Heidegger's re-configuration of the Hölderlinian hymns is that, notwithstanding his blanket rejection of allegory, symbol, simile, and example as attesting to representational thinking (GA 53, 17–19), his own reading tacitly avails itself of these interpretive structures. He treats the poem as a cryptogram to be decoded by the thinker, who, in virtue of his special relationship to the poet out of the *essential* Being of language, holds the key to its supposed correspondences. These are taken to be uniformly onto-historical; the autofiguration of poetry, in particular (as distinct from its own problematizing of its onto-historical role), is suppressed.

Furthermore, Heidegger largely suppresses the figure of the Asian East in "Andenken" and "Der Ister," and in Hölderlin's poetry and prose in general, in favor of a binary schema interlinking Germany and Greece. His reading of the two hymns assimilates the journey of the seafarers in "Andenken" (a journey "to Indian people") to the thematization of Eastern origins in "Der Ister":

Wir singen aber vom Indus her
Fernangekommen und
Vom Alpheus . . .

and:

Ich meine, er müsse kommen
Von Osten.
Vieles wäre
Zu sagen davon . . .[20]

The Indus, Heidegger notes, is the stream (the poetic spirit) that "made the original homeland of the parents homelike and founded the first dwelling" (GA 4, 140). The poetic reference here is presumably to the Vedic hymns. The place of parental provenance, however, is for Heidegger the "decisive locality," where a course of wandering reverses itself and turns homeward, orienting itself, first of all, toward Greece (the Alpheus). Heidegger does not consider the question of why and how a journey from "Bourdeaux" (Hölderlin's conscious archaism), which stands for ancient Greece, should proceed westward (driven by the northeasterly wind) to "Indian people."[21] He points out only that Greece, as the other of the homeland, is what is glimpsed and greeted first but is also what, in the leave taking of departure (toward the eastern turning-point), receives the last greeting (GA 4, 141).

Hölderlin's own fivefold historical schema, as painstakingly outlined by Jean-François Marquet,[22] describes the figure of an infinite interconnection (∞). The historical sequence proceeds from (1) the Asian beginning of an immediate, initial union with the divine, through (2) loss and separation, or the withdrawal of the gods, to (3) the Greek experience of the heavenly fire, and onwards through (4) the blinding brought about by this excess, toward (5) a possible Hesperian conciliation. Since Greece is situated here at the juncture of the chiasm which separates and conjoins antiquity and modernity, East and West, it is the turning-point and the place of decision. This turning-point holds a median position and conjoins Orient and Occident while marking their difference. Such a differential union of Orient and Occident is indicated (in terms of the iconography of the conjunction of solar and lunar energies) in an enigmatic sequence of verses from "Der Ister," which seems to baffle even Heidegger's interpretive ingenuity:

> . . . Aber wie? Ein Zeichen braucht es
> Nichts anderes, schlecht und recht, damit es Sonn
> und Mond trag' im Gemüth', untrennbar,
> Und fortgeh, Tag und Nacht auch . . .[23]

Heidegger—quite apart from dissevering Hölderlin's thought from its own historico-political context (which is that of the French Revolution)—interprets its figure of infinite interconnection through a linear, quasi-dialectical, *arche-telic* schema that, paradoxically, is put in the service of a surpassing of metaphysics. Finally, he disregards the tentative and tenuous character of Hölderlin's own interpretive constructs. There is no echo, in Heidegger's reading, of the poet's awareness that "the mythology of reason" which he, along with his philosophical colleagues, had hoped to found proved to be one whose "despoiled landscape," as Marquet notes, was "at once constructed and ruined by the same unsustainable lightning stroke."[24]

III

Heidegger reads Hölderlin's call, in the third strophe of "Andenken," for a "fragrant beaker full of the dark light" as an articulation of the poet's mediating role (shielding mortals from the destructive splendor of the heavenly fire). He proceeds to complement the oxymoron of the dark light with one of his own, interpreting the poet's desire for the sweetness of slumber "under shadows" or "among shades" (*unter Schatten*) as the "sober drunkenness" of poetic exaltation. He is particularly insensitive to Hölderlin's consummate conjoining of Hades and Dionysos, of the tropes of festive repose with suggestions of death. For this reason, Heidegger's reading also neglects the antagonistic force of the stressed *nicht* (not) in the ensuing verses:

> Nicht ist es gut,
> Seellos von sterblichen

> Gedanken zu seyn. Doch gut
> Ist ein Gespräch . . .[25]

The force of this "not" has perhaps its closest poetic analogue in Keats's insistent repudiation of the massed and compelling figures of death in the first strophe of "Ode on Melancholy." Whereas Keats, however, moves quickly to resolve the tension, Hölderlin's statement ("Nicht ist es gut . . .") retrenches itself in irresoluble ambiguity; for it can be read either as cautioning against having one's soul bereft *of* mortal thoughts, or against being bereft of soul *by* mortal thoughts.[26] Either reading, however, returns the poet to the community of human conversation and to commemorating the "days of love" and heroic deeds.

While the poet is thus called back to his proper task, the friends—"Bellarmin and his companion"—who should share the conversation are distant. They have taken to the sea to "bring together, like painters, what there is of beauty upon the earth," at the cost of solitude, hardship, and deprivation. Heidegger understands these verses as indicating Hölderlin's surpassing of the "*Hyperion*-stage" (indicated by the figure of Bellarmin), as well as the important difference between the poetic "law" of seeking the source and the projective, hypothetical (and thus metaphysical and proto-technical) labors of the seafarers, to whom, however, the poet remains bound in friendship. What articulates itself here, in Heidegger's thematization, is the divergence of *poiēsis* and *technē* from out of their original bond.[27]

One can then read the origin and source as *poiēsis* itself (thus de-literalizing the "homecoming" of the poet), in that poetic configuration is the very *oriri* of manifestation and thus of the phenomenal richness which fascinates the "painters." Heidegger, of course, understands poetic configuration as the *ess*ential character of language itself and hence remarks, in "The Origin of the Work of Art," that "language itself is poesy (*Dichtung*) in the *ess*ential sense," and that therefore poetry remains closest of all the arts to this *ess*ential poetizing.[28]

This line of thought suggests that the seafarers of "Andenken" should be understood not just as "other poets," as Heidegger understands them, but as the thinkers of German Idealism (including perhaps poets like Novalis and Schiller). As Jean-Luc Nancy points out (in the person of Bellarmin writing to Selenion), these thinkers shared the exigency (inaugurated by Kant) of thinking the One no longer as self-identical and universal but as constituting itself in process and multiplicity, and thus in its own undoing.[29]

Their labors of unification resist the self-relinquishing desire for annihilation (*Todeslust*) that, for Hölderlin, is often connoted by the figure of the streams flowing into the sea; they gather the richness of phenomenal presence into a "phenomenology." Hölderlin suggests that such a labor, which is under the aegis of what Heidegger calls *thesis*, or which might be described as a search for a present origin of presence, must forget at the same time as it recollects, and that it cannot, therefore, found what abides. Love, on the other hand (thought of perhaps as having the priority to spirit which Schelling accords it), devotes itself assiduously to fixating and thus to abiding; but it remains in a receptive role and is incapable of founding.

What, then, is the distinctive character of a poetic founding of that which abides? What abides, first of all, is not what can be set up in the manner of *thesis*, reified, installed as *archē* or *telos*, or absolutized. It is the empty and differential origin of manifestation. As Heidegger emphasizes in "The Origin of the Work of Art," the truth worked by the work is an opening up which allows *Dasein* to disengage itself from the rapture (*Berückung*) that habitually keeps it caught up among beings. It thus brings about a displacement (*Entrückung, Verrückung*), which, in the very openness of beings, allows Being to reveal itself as open and empty. The truth of the art-work thought of as this power of displacement (which Heidegger here calls also by the Fichtean term *Anstoss*) is not something which thought can set up nor love cling to. The work can work displacement because, in its created form, it withdraws from explanatory schemata into the enigma of its sheer "that-ness" and "suchness":

> ... That which has the character of *Ereignis*, that the work is as this work, is what throws the work ahead of itself and has constantly thrown it about itself. The more *essentially* the work opens itself, the more radiant becomes the singularity of this: that it is rather than is not ... In the bringing-forth of the work, there lies the offering (*Darbringen*) of the "that it is." (GA 5, 53)

This is why Heidegger's path of inquiry in "The Origin of the Work of Art" must proceed from the art-work to the thing, rather than vice versa (as originally attempted); for it is the art-work which gives access to the "Earth"-character of the thing, its enigmatic suchness. The latter, Heidegger finds, at the conclusion of a tortuous aporetic, is foreclosed by the philosophemes of the Western intellectual tradition.

What enables the art-work to transpose *Dasein* into an awareness of the dynamic space of emptiness as the place and event of *oriri* is the work's own differential or "polemic" structure, as well as its differential origination in the reciprocity between "creating" and "preserving." Whereas the former is the non-thetic crystallizing of finite configuration out of emptiness, the latter is the safekeeping of the work's non-thetic character and displacing power.

Heidegger here takes up the thought that Nancy characterizes as the sustained and crucial thought of Hölderlin: the thought of a containment of the infinite in the finite, which is not a matter of identity or coincidence, yet is such as to leave no outside and nothing, therefore, to be dialectically retrieved and completed:

> Infinite life does not follow *upon* life and does not overtake *it*. But life succeeds and exceeds itself as such; and it overtakes within life . . . [This thought] thinks the finite being as the paradoxical, the untenable circumscription of the infinite . . . The infinite overtakes on the inside: this is the whole Kantian problematic of the "supra-sensible faculty" of the infinite, which is to say that the thought of finitude *is* the thought of the *sublime*.[30]

For Hölderlin, a poetic founding of what abides is ultimately this very concretion and crystallization of the infinite, its untenable inscription in a finite configuration, which becomes the conjunction of excess and lack. The "firm letter," nevertheless, must hold its own against the destructive pull into the boundless.

Heidegger himself, stressing that the source, in its de-rivation, exceeds itself and is thus not self-sufficient, characterizes the origin as both excess and lack;[31] yet he seeks immediately to embed the source in its hidden "ground," which, whatever its darkness, stands firm. To show forth (*zeigen*) the origin, he insists, is to establish it firmly and festively (*festigen, fest-stecken*) in its *essential* ground, which is the holy. Such a showing, which renders festive and firm, is what he understands by a poetic founding, which also founds itself by abiding in a nearness to the origin that keeps open the dimension of distance:

> The origin, through a rendering firm of its ground which returns into itself, allows the farthest distance to originate, and with it the possibility of a pure nearness which sustains distance. The origin can be shown forth only in that such showing, as the return, originated by the origin, allows itself to become an approach to the origin. (GA 4, 147)

Instead of the untenable Hölderlinian dislocation of the infinite into the finite, which alone can show it forth, but which is thus eroded, Heidegger resorts to the countermove: he seeks to restore the finite to its *essential* ground. Although this ground is thought as the empty space of the Differing, in which nothing can take root and entrench itself in abiding presence, Heidegger's move of grounding remains the founding act characteristic of the thinker, not the poet.

Despite his general fondness for "polemic" unification, Heidegger understands the relationship between poet and thinker as complementary rather than tensional.

Poetic founding, which requires recourse to "the highest," is what "consecrates the ground"; but such consecration does not yet accomplish the building necessary for full human dwelling. To "hold firm" upon the consecrated ground and to build upon it brings into play what is "most severe," the lucid articulation of thought. A thinking that does not establish itself upon the consecrated ground of the holy, Heidegger observes, can amount to no more than "the self-installation of the forgetting of the ultimate truth that even nothingness does not *essentially* obtain (*west*) without Being" (GA 4, 149). Such a thinking is therefore prone to nihilism as its ultimate danger. It is curious that the reciprocity between poetizing and thinking here outlined constitutes, in effect, a modernization of the medieval relationship of philosophy to theology, the relationship of the "handmaiden." Through this modernization, furthermore, the reciprocity legitimates Heidegger's characteristic historico-political deflection; for he concludes that the "abiding" thus founded prepares the historical locality in which the *Menschentum* of the Germans must first of all learn to become at home, so as to begin to dwell in the "whiling" of a destinal balance. This task devolves upon the Germans because they are, supposedly, the neo-Greek people of poets and thinkers. Heidegger, in this context, does not hesitate to resort to the disturbing quasi-religious rhetoric of ritual sacrifice: the poet, in being destined to the *essence* of poethood, is elected to become "a sacrifice of the firstborn" (*Erstlingsopfer*) and finds himself, in such destining, "greeted in an originary way" (GA 4, 150).

The "fault" in Heidegger's exegeses is not only what Fynsk calls (with reference to the Hölderlinian figure of Oedipus) the "Oedipal fault" of excessive interpretation[32]—a disregard for poetic finitude—but also an astonishing neglect, as concerns the relationship between poetizing and thinking, of "polemic" unification in favor of a complementarity that, in the end, legitimates totalization. This totalization is at once—in a com-plicated and also conflated manner—textual, "spiritual," and, even where it opposes itself to the politics of National Socialism, historico-political. With respect to Hölderlin's "Andenken," it neglects the sharp divergence in the trajectories of poet(s) and thinker(s) (significantly, it is Heidegger who speaks of these in the singular), who set out from "the lofty tip" of the French/Greek shore. Whereas the latter seek to explore and assimilate the originary in its remoteness, the former return to a place of provenance, which is, however, constituted by and thus dislocated through commemoration. This singular reception of the infinite in the finite particular cannot legitimate an historical instauration.

The thinker can, at best, respond to it by a "preserving" gesture that safeguards its unsettling power and refuses to annex it, thus letting the text originate as art-work and restoring it to the Differing, which repudiates totalization. The poetic text then configures itself in dehiscence, in multiple "throws" and counter-throws, which privilege no singular inception (*Anfang*) or beginning.

5

◆

Mnemosyne's Death and the Failure of Mourning

... mein Herz wird
Untrügbarer Kristall an dem
Das Licht sich prüfet ...

Hölderlin, "Vom Abgrund nemlich ..."

... my heart becomes
undeceiving crystal by which
the light is tested ...

The inner dynamics of history, as Heidegger understands it, are essentially poetic and philosophical, in that the poet "institutes" (*stiftet*) history, whereas the thinker "founds" (*gründet*) it by theoretically elaborating an epoch's self-understanding.[1] Insofar as historical configurations are thus traced to a reciprocity between poetizing and thinking, they spring from language construed as "the power to bring to word." In the contemporary modality of unconcealment, however, language has become instrumentalized and technicized and is rendered subservient to information and communication. The momentous change signalled by this transformation of language is, Heidegger holds, a change in the very modality of unconcealment: the "gentle law" (*Ge-setz*) of manifestation (akin to Anaximander's *taxis* of time) becomes occluded by the totalizing posure (*Ge-stell*) of technicity, which is not, for Heidegger, a mere infatuation with technological power but rather the very nature of evil:

> Everything which is dis-enfitted (*das Ungefüge*) brings confusion; confusion creates errancy; and errancy is openness for treachery. Together with the dis-enfitted, the nature of evil (*das Bösartige*) is set free. Evil is not merely the morally bad; it is not at all a fault or shortcoming among beings, but is Being itself as misfitting mischief (*Unfug*) and treachery.

When the Enfitting does not hold sway, the fundamental modes of Being, the elements, are not balanced in the freedom of their proper *essentiality*.[2]

As this passage indicates, Heidegger does not regard the displacement of the Enfitting, or "law" (*Fug*, *Ge-setz*), by the rampant totalization of *Ge-stell* as a mere human aberration, a fault to be castigated and eradicated. Rather, Being itself, as the self-withholding granting of historical configurations (a granting which engages language and requires human participation), brings about "danger." As Heidegger remarks in "The Question Concerning Technology":

The destiny of unconcealment is, in and of itself, not some danger or other, but *the* danger.

If destiny prevails, however, in the manner of the posure (*Ge-stell*), it is the utmost danger.[3]

Heidegger is prepared to acknowledge that danger, like the granting of manifestation, the disclosive power of language, and indeed the very *essence* of *alētheia*, is profoundly ambiguous: it carries its opposite within itself in a tension that remains without dialectical resolution. Even technicity as the "utmost danger," which threatens to reduce all presencing to mere disponible resource (*Bestand*), remains "ambiguous in an exalted sense"; and this ambiguity is linked, for Heidegger, to "the mystery of all unconcealment."[4] Since danger itself gives rise to and sustains "that which saves," Heidegger experiences no attrition of hope. The specter of despair is transformed into a consciousness of destinal or "spiritual" mission, which calls upon the thinker to heed the word of the poet who speaks to a "destitute time." This poet is, of course, Hölderlin, and the reciprocity between poet and thinker which Heidegger strives to inaugurate is to bring about a new historical instauration.

Heidegger's reading of Hölderlin is, as he often remarks, divorced from the concerns of literary scholarship precisely because it stands under the aegis of such a hoped-for destinal transformation, which is also to bring to fruition the unconsummated promise of the Greek beginnings of Western thought. This thought-structure informs, in particular, Heidegger's reading of the tropes of greeting, sending, celebration, and commemoration in Hölderlin's hymn "Andenken."[5] In the intellectual landscape thus mapped out, Hölderlin's last hymn, "Mnemosyne," closely linked to "Andenken" through the thematic of commemoration, marks the consummate "intensification" rather than the dismantling of these structures. As Anselm Haverkamp remarks, in a passage which goes against the grain of Heidegger's self-perception by re-installing him securely in Hölderlin scholarship:

Hölderlin interpretation, especially under Heidegger's imprimatur, has seen the close relation of "Andenken" and "Mnemosyne" more in terms of celebration than of mourning and has consequently identified in "Mnemosyne" not the anticlimax ("regression") of "Andenken" but its climax ("intensification").[6]

This deflection in favor of "celebration," or, perhaps better, commemorative retrieval (reclaiming the Greek past for the Occidental future), leaves Heidegger in a paradoxical position. On the one hand, he is convinced that "Mnemosyne" belongs to a constellation of poems crucial for grasping Hölderlin's poetic thought, and that its reading must be guided by that of "Andenken"; but on the other, he remains quite unable to undertake such a reading, which continues to be deferred with unfulfilled promissory notes.[7]

I

With a characteristic interpretive gesture (which Allemann has criticized),[8] Heidegger focuses his reading of Hölderlin on singularized significant *words*, among which, in the "Andenken" lectures, "greeting" and "festivity" are prominent. He understands the "greeting" which the poet entrusts to the wind of passage as a figure of the "sameness" of poetizing and thinking. What is important, he notes, is to bring the movements of Hölderlin's wind "into relation to poetizing and thinking and [to] grasp, out of this relation, the wind and breath and thus also 'spirit'" (GA 52, 55). The sameness of poetizing and thinking lies in their release of presencing to show itself in its *essential* provenance out of the Differing. Since the gesture of greeting (as distinct from grasping) shows respect for the Differing, it is characterized by an attuned responsiveness to the originary greeting, which, for Heidegger, is the way "the holy" addresses itself to man (GA 52, 71). It is, of course, of the essence of greeting to be responsive; but the response here is "regressive" in a curious sense: instead of extending itself outward to the unknown Other, it seeks the withdrawn source. Heidegger, indeed, likens this movement to that of the Hölderlinian stream (the Ister), which, in its approach to the sea, suddenly flows backwards and resurges from the source.[9] By this recursive movement, such greeting is capable of relating Hesperian civilization to what Hölderlin thinks of as the "Oriental fire" of ancient Greece, and thus to retrieve for futurity the unconsummated anticipation of the Differing in early Greek thought. A poetic saying and thinking which accomplishes such greeting has the character of commemoration or *Andenken* and is capable of spanning the desolate reaches of a time out of joint.

Originary greeting, on the other hand, for Heidegger takes the form of what he calls, in the words of Hölderlin's Rhine hymn, the bridal feast of divinities and mortals. As a mutual self-entrustment out of a shared *essential* origin, these nuptial festivities constitute *Ereignis*, opening up and configuring an epochal span of history (GA 52, 77). Since, as Heidegger insists, it was Greek poetry and thinking which prepared the "early festivities," an antici- pation of festivities still to come must take its bearings from a remembrance of ancient Greece, which cannot be allowed to degenerate into mere nostal- gia or mimetic renewal. Such remembrance requires, rather, that the true character of the festive be first brought into view.

Festivities, Heidegger points out, must be prepared for by "days of celebration" (*Feiertage*). Celebration here consists in relinquishing one's habitual, "workaday," and inattentive modes of construing reality, thus allowing "the unaccustomed" to assert itself in the manner of perplexity as to what it means "that there are beings and not, rather, nothing, that things are, and we are in their midst . . ." (GA 52, 64).

Such wonder (notwithstanding the fact that it has also ushered in the entire course of Western metaphysics) effects a break in the tightening stranglehold of *Ge-stell* and thus allows one to heed the "gentle law" which orders without suppressing difference (whether "ontic" or "ontological"). Heidegger links the articulation effected by the "gentle law" to festive play and dance:

> But freeing oneself from the habitual for the unaccustomed proper is not a reeling into the boundless, but rather a bonding to what is of the essence and to the hidden pliancy and rule of beings. The freely reverberating bond to the rule and the unfolding of the wealth of the free possibilities of the rule-governed stemming from this reverberation—this is the essential Being of play. When man himself, in the controlled unity of his form, enters into play, dance originates . . . (GA 52, 67).

Festivity is, then, heedful participation in, and free conformance to, the differential play of manifestation. For an historical people, in Heidegger's view, this amounts to a welcoming acceptance of its own historical mission in its provenance from the "missive" character of manifestation.

As Allemann points out, it is precisely the bridal feast, as the achievement of destinal balance (*ausgeglichenes Schicksal*) that constitutes, for Heidegger, the opening up of the intermediary or differential dimension in Hölderlin's poetry.[10] In his lecture course on "Andenken," Heidegger thematizes this intermediary dimension in two ways: as interlocution (*Gespräch*) and as dream.

The thematic of dream is developed entirely in relation to (if not, indeed, in interlocution with) ancient Greece. The character of dream, as Heidegger delineates it, is ambiguous. Dream may be understood, on the one hand, as the "cradling" enchantment of the "golden dreams" Hölderlin speaks of in "Andenken," which is to say, as the trope of a sheltering in the balance of "the ownmost." For ancient Greece, the ownmost was what Hölderlin calls the "Oriental fire," which Heidegger interprets as the pure radiance of *phainesthai*. To those who rest cradled in this element, beings are not manifest as intrinsically and ultimately real, but as issuing from and again drawn into the empty heart of manifestation. In the dream-dimension as thus understood, Being's withdrawal appears, subverting all in-sistence on and clinging to intrinsic realities.

The other Greek understanding of the dreamlike articulates itself, Heidegger finds, in Pindar's *Eighth Pythian Ode*, where man's transient life is described as a shadow's dream.[11] It is not, however, sheer transience that relegates mortals to an "utmost absencing into the lightless" (GA 52, 115), but rather their insistence upon the inherent reality of what presences—their natural resistance, that is, to the "cradling" aspect of dream just discussed. The second (Pindaric) aspect of dream is thus an obscuring of the pure radiance of *phainesthai* and of the withdrawal at its core; it brings to pass the radical oblivion which Heidegger, in the *Parmenides* lectures, calls *Vergessung*.[12]

In both these aspects, the dreamlike marks the in-between of the Differing, but it does so in contrary modes that point to the contrariety, or *Gegenwendigkeit*, of *alētheia*. Heidegger conjoins these aspects (without lessening their tension) in that he characterizes destinal transition, with reference to Hölderlin's 1800 essay "Das Werden im Vergehen" ("Becoming in Perishing"),[13] as a de-realizing "idealization" of what was previously taken for real and for granted. In being "idealized," this is now consigned to remembrance and yields to the sheer expectancy of the "possible." Dream, then, as the de-realization and de-literalization that happens in destinal transition, undoes its own aspect of *Vergessung* and becomes an expectant or, as Heidegger calls it, with reference to the third version of "Mnemosyne," "prophetic" dreaming which welcomes the Differing.

Heidegger's thematization of interlocution (*Gespräch*) in the "Andenken" lectures takes up the issue of friendship. What opens up the intermediary dimension here is the encounter (*Entgegnung*) between divinities and mortals, who, in speaking their *essential* Being to one another, allow the granting withdrawal to stand revealed, in the mode of absence, within the space of interlocution. It is Heidegger's insistence on thinking this granting withdrawal, which is "the holy," as emptiness or as the Spared, which motivates his distortions—criticized by Michel Haar—of the Hölderlinian figure of "the god." Haar points out that this god, notwithstanding the difficulty of naming, grasping, or celebrating him in his purity, is neither "empty" nor withdrawn but manifests "incontestable and overabundant presence."[14]

Since "the holy," for Heidegger, cannot be directly said or brought to presence, its oblique saying, through the words of the poet, must be prepared for by the mortal celebration of what Hölderlin calls the "days of love" and of heroic deeds. Like the privileged aspect of dream, interlocution is fundamentally remembrance or *Erinnerung*, a "becoming intimate with what is of the essence (*dem Wesenhaften*), as what always already essentially obtains" (GA 52, 161). The "*essential conversation*" of mortals who commemorate heroism and love is, on Heidegger's understanding, the basis and the very form of friendship only in that it is an "anticipatory preparation of the heavenly interlocution into which mortals must already be drawn" (GA 52, 162).

Friendship is here conceived as essentially a form of truth. Its aletheic character neglects Spinoza's insight that man is God to man, as well as the Graeco-Roman and political model of friendship (based on reciprocity), in favor of what Derrida describes as the "heterology, asymmetry, and infinity" of non-reciprocity and non-requital.[15] For Heidegger, such asymmetry has positive import, for he sees mortals as first of all oriented toward "the holy" and bound into the configuration of the Fourfold, rather than as being in the situation of human encounter. He therefore hears Hölderlin's question, "Wo aber sind die Freunde?" ("Where, however, are the friends?"), which opens the fourth strophe of "Andenken," as a question concerning "the *essence* of friendship yet to come" (GA 52, 169), a friendship which exceeds human communion. The poet's bereaved singularization is, for him, the mark attesting to "the respect of the one first sacrificed before the sacrifice" (GA 52, 170).[16] This sacrifice sets the poet apart from those who, in the manner of the Idealist "seafarers," dedicate themselves to a dialectical exploration of what is alien, and remain unable to accomplish "the transition into the homelike." These explorers, Heidegger concludes, are incapable of understanding either the alien or the homelike, for they lack the courage to accept "the essential-original poverty" [of thought] and to turn toward what is "simple and originary" (GA 52, 176).

Derrida, who locates the initial fracture of the reciprocal or symmetrical model of friendship in Montaigne, and who sees it as the dissociation of friendship from historicity and exemplarity, asks whether this change can be considered peculiarly Judeo-Christian.[17] Turned back upon Heidegger, Derrida's question opens up a scene of labyrinthine complexities. On the one hand, as Habermas observes, Heidegger's engagement with Hölderlin's poetry signals, beginning in 1929, "a *neopagan* turn that pushed Christian themes into the background, in favor of a mythologizing recourse to the archaic . . .";[18] but on the other, this turn comes out of a rethinking of *historicity*, which, as Habermas also notes, transforms the play of "invariant possibilities of Being" into "the story of a fall."[19] Notwithstanding Heidegger's infatuation with Hölderlin, his aletheic understanding of interlocution and friendship functions in the context of the Judeo-Christian thought-structures of fall, redemption, and the expectancy of a new advent of the divine in history. To complicate this Graeco-Judeo-Christian amalgam still further, Heidegger literalizes the Hölderlinian figure of Germania and bestows upon the German nation the elect status of a chosen people, while insisting, at the same time, that this status reflects Germany's linguistic, philosophical, and poetic kinship to ancient Greece.[20]

Although the figure of the singularized, self-sacrificing poet, who, in his uncertain wandering, guides the chosen people in a time of destinal transition, now replaces Heidegger's crude earlier figure of the spiritual and political leader (*Führer*),[21] the figure of the poet is clearly messianic. With respect to the thinker, the poet is a precursor, a voice crying in the wilderness, while his asymmetrical relation to the "seafarers" recalls Christ's relationship to the Apostles. These complex changes are not adequately summed up by Habermas's diagnosis that, beginning in 1936, Heidegger's thinking shifts from an apocalyptic mood to a messianic hope of salvation.[22] Rather, a persistent, complicated, and uncanny conflation of both apocalyptic and messianic paradigms with Greek thought structures characterizes Heidegger's intellectual vision, and the poisonous brew of this conflation inflames his politics.

While this conclusion lends new urgency to the seemingly arcane task of interpreting Heidegger's relation to the god of Hölderlin, the present study follows a different track by taking up the issue of tragedy and mourning.

The mortal conversation which commemorates love and heroic deeds is, for Heidegger, (in contrast to mere idle talk or *Geschwätz*) a "poetizing conversation" that can be articulated in the lyric, hymnic, epic, or tragic modes (see GA 52, 164f). The essential task of poetizing is (in congruence with the work of dream and festivity) to accomplish remembrance (*Erinnerung, Andenken*). For this reason, Heidegger describes "the festive" as "the ground for both joy and mourning," insisting that these must not be regarded as mere human psychisms but as "fundamental feeling-tones" (*Grundstimmungen*), which allow the soundless voice of Being to be heard (GA 52, 71f). Reflecting here on Hölderlin's devotion—as translator, dramatist, and theoretician—to Greek tragedy, Heidegger observes:

> Although Hölderlin did not, in a thinking way (*denkerisch*), reflect in such a manner on the essence of attunement (*Stimmung*), he knows well what is meant here in a poetic way (*dichterisch*); and he also brought this knowledge poetically to word, relating it, at the same time, to the highest poetry, [which is] Greek tragedy. (GA 52, 72; the shifts in tense are Heidegger's.)

It is surprising, given Heidegger's usual privileging of Hölderlin's lyric poetry, that he comes close, in this discussion, to agreeing with Lacoue-Labarthe's insistence that the Hölderlin who must today be interrogated is, above all, the dramatist and theoretician of Greek tragedy.[23] He explicitly refers his listeners or readers to Hölderlin's enigmatic "Remarks" on Sophoclean tragedy:

> Hölderlin, rather, experiences in the poetry of Sophocles the Other, that which Essentially-Was (*das Gewesene*); and for this reason it becomes necessary [for him] to translate *Oedipus Tyrannus* and *Antigone*; for this reason he struggles to deliver himself of the "Remarks" on both these tragedies—which "Remarks," indeed, belong among those treasures difficult of access about which the Germans know nothing . . . as long as they consider themselves able to invent their own *essentiality*, instead of truly discovering it in the word of history proper (*der eigentlichen Geschichte*). (GA 52, 73)

Why, then, does Heidegger find himself unable to read Hölderlin's last hymn, "Mnemosyne," which focuses on the very issues of tragedy, remembrance, and mourning? Why can he not amalgamate this hymn with its immediate precursor, "Andenken," which opens up, for him, the full scope of Hölderlin's poetic thought of remembrance? What is the resistance which "Mnemosyne" offers to the interpretive moves of Heidegger's "elucidations"; and what, if it can be identified, is its significance?

II

In sharp contrast to the almost contemporaneous hymn "Andenken," which recognizes the poet as one who institutes "that which abides," "Mnemosyne," in its third and final version, speaks of the death of Mnemosyne, or Remembrance, the mother of the Muses, and thus of the failure of poetic commemoration. In the first strophe of the hymn (the strophe most radically altered in the three versions), Hölderlin speaks of the Law of the all-consuming and all-transmuting heavenly fire into which all things must enter, "snake-like, / Prophetic, dreaming upon / The hills of heaven." The figure of the snake calls to mind both the Pentecostal tongues of flame from heaven and the chthonic realm that Hölderlin, in his "Remarks on Oedipus," calls "the eccentric sphere of the dead" (FA 16, 251). The Law of the fire which overtakes all things (in a manner reminiscent both of the Heraclitean fire and of Stoic *ekpyrōsis*) seems to be caught in ambiguity: on the one hand, it is a "prophetic" law of transmutation, but on the other, it threatens to transport man into what Hölderlin calls, in the "Remarks on Antigone," "the ever-living, unwritten wilderness" (FA 16, 413). In "Mnemosyne," the poet affirms that "much" must be salvaged from the imminent conflagration:

> . . . Und vieles
> Wie auf Schultern eine
> Last von Scheitern ist
> Zu behalten . . .[24]

Heidegger, in his essay "Das Gedicht," cites these verses to indicate the abyssal failure of ground experienced by the poets, who announce "the remoteness of the god drawing near" (GA 4, 190). Since he isolates the verses from their context, he pays no attention to the fire imagery, nor yet to the impossibility of saving a load of firewood (*Scheitern*) from the encompassing flames. These flames threaten also to consume the one who carries the load, and to change the articulated manifold (*vieles*) into a unitary totality (*eine*, stressed by the linebreak) through sheer destruction. The imminent failure of the effort to "preserve" or "remember" (a common if figurative sense of *behalten*) is further indicated by the fact that *scheitern*, heard as a verbal infinitive rather than as the declension of a noun, denotes failing and coming to grief. What one must carry on one's shoulders becomes, then, a burden of failure.

Hölderlin, indeed, immediately adduces the obstacles which resist and frustrate preservation and remembrance: in being drawn into conflagration, the "captive elements" go wildly astray; and above all, "a longing" tends ever toward "the boundless." Although the injunction to retain "much" is immediately reiterated and is reinforced by the emphatic statement that faithfulness now is sheer necessity ("und Noth die Treue"), the strophe concludes with the admission (introduced by the third reversing and qualifying "but") that "we" refuse to look forward and backward, preferring instead to let ourselves be cradled in ahistoric immediacy as in a boat adrift at sea.

If the task of tragedy is the task of purification (symbolized by fire), such that, as Lacoue-Labarthe puts it, tragedy, in an "echo of Aristotelian *catharsis* . . . represents the infinite separation of that pure monstrosity or enormity (*hybris*) that is the infinite collusion of man and God,"[25] the accomplishment of this task is far from assured. One can agree with Lacoue-Labarthe that the interruption that Hölderlin calls the "caesura" is the very concept of discontinuous or, in Heideggerian parlance, epochal historicity; but this interruption (which affirms the "metric" law of tragedy) is perpetually and intrinsically menaced by obliteration. By the force of sheer tragic transport, such obliteration pulls man into the boundless or the undifferentiated, which is to say, into totalization, thus marking the failure of poetic commemoration.

Haverkamp reads the question, "Wie aber liebes?" ("But how [about] what is loved?"),[26] which opens the second strophe, as a response to the concluding verses of the first strophe, which, in the hymn's first and second versions, affirm that "there comes into its own/ What is true":[27]

> With this syntactic construction in mind, the question at the beginning of the second strophe reads as a question of whether love is bound to take place. Where, in the first strophe, we read "das Wahre" as the asserted

truth, in the second strophe we read "Liebes" [not capitalized by Höl-derlin] as a loving in question.[28]

Such an interpretation is not only somewhat simplistic but, more impor-tantly, cannot give a reason as to why Hölderlin, who valued poetic craftsmanship, should have retained the opening question in the third version, in which the first strophe no longer contains any reference to "the true." Although the second strophe remains, on the whole, close to the earlier versions, the verses

> . . . und es girren
> Verloren in der Luft die Lerchen und unter dem Tage waiden
> Wohlangeführt die Schafe des Himmels.

are replaced by the following:

> . . . gut sind nemlich
> Hat gegenredig die Seele
> Ein Himmlisches verwundet, die Tageszeichen.[29]

Other more notable changes are the introduction of the adjective *heimatlich* (homelike) in the third verse, and of the notion of *Zorn* (wrath) toward the end of the strophe. This latter notion, in Hölderlin's late diction, stands for the impassioned effacement of differentiation, notably of the difference which divides man and divinity.[30]

The question, "Wie aber liebes?" is better read as an echo of the preceding affirmation that "much" (*vieles*) is to be retained. What is beloved is the peaceable articulation of human dwelling in its well-ordered dailiness. Thus the simple differentiation between the "sunshine / Upon the ground and dry dust" and the cool "homelike shade of the forests" resists the destructive pull into the unformed and boundless. Hölderlin begins the next sentence and verse with an emphatic, explanatory *denn* (for), which replaces the noncommittal "and" of the earlier versions:

> Denn Schnee, wie Majenblumen
> Das Edelmütige, wo
> Es seie, bedeutend, glänzet auf
> Der grünen Wiese
> Der Alpen, hälftig . . .[31]

Although the alpine meadows, conjoining snow and flowers amid the new green, maintain the "halving" of proper differentiation, the kinship between flowers and snow, which are both ephemerally resplendent, indicates the precariousness of this separation. The risk in such a halving is pointedly stated in Hölderlin's "Remarks on *Antigone*":

The most daring moment in the course of a day or in a work of art is when the spirit of time and nature, the heavenly which seizes man, and the object which interests him, are most wildly opposed to one another; for the sensuous object reaches only as far as one half, but spirit *awakens most powerfully* where *the second half* begins. In this moment, man needs to hold himself steady the most . . . (FA 16, 412)[32]

As Klaus Düsing points out, both *Oedipus* and *Antigone* are, for Hölderlin, tragedies of a time in transition (*Zeitwende*), when the established moral, religious, or intellectual order is disintegrating and a new order is not yet apparent.[33] Such times are fraught with the greatest risk, and certain individuals, caught up in the tragic *nefas* of arrogating to themselves a divine, illuminating vision, must suffer their tragic undoing, so that differentiation and measure may be maintained. The "patriotic turning" (*vaterländische Umkehr*) mandated in such times restores a people to the earth and to its finite historical identity. Although such a turning is not patriotic in any nationalistic or ideological sense, it may, Hölderlin thinks, constrain someone who is politically uncommitted to become patriotic, in the narrower sense, and to become, as an agitator and revolutionary, one who is "present in infinite form, the religious, political, and moral [form] of his fatherland" (FA 16, 410).[34] It is partly for this reason that the patriotic turning may issue into tragic destinies; and furthermore, it threatens with sheer desolation (*Wildnis*). The bearing of Hölderlin's remarks on Heidegger's political identification certainly deserves to be pondered.

In the second strophe of "Mnemosyne," the figure of the cross follows immediately upon that of the divided meadow. A "wanderer" (the traditional figure of the poet) travels "wrathfully" and "distantly divining" with the unnamed "other one" (who, following Haverkamp, may be Rousseau), speaking of the cross. The poem alludes here to the alpine custom of erecting crosses by the wayside in memory of those who have died upon the trail. The crosses thus set up (*gesetzt*) commemorate also the law (*Gesetz*) of their perishing, as well as symbolizing the supervenience of Christianity upon pagan antiquity. As Allemann points out, however, Hölderlin experiences Christ himself as one who could not restrain the impassioned excess of soul, which tore him into the boundless, away from the earth.[35] Through his "wrath" and his speaking "of the cross," the poet is linked to two modalities of excess: that of the heroes of antiquity and that of Christ. The perplexed question, "Aber was ist diss?," ("But what is this?") that concludes the second strophe constitutes a call for (self)interpretation.

The elegiac opening verses of the third strophe (which Beissner regards as the germ of the poem)[36] do not immediately respond to this call:

Am Feigenbaum ist mein
Achilles mir gestorben[37]

The fig tree here is not only the Homeric fig tree by the walls of Troy but also the fig tree of the New Testament, whose new shoots announce the ripeness of time (and thus an imminent transformation);[38] it recalls also the fig tree of "Andenken," which grows in the courtyard's shelter. Among the complex meanings thus set into play, one can single out, as most prominent, the linking of Christ to the heroes of antiquity (as already discussed), the perishing of a nearly invincible hero with the advent of a new time, as well as a re-reading of "Andenken" in loss and mourning. The poet's self-identification with the figure of Achilles is brought home by the emphatic "my" and "mine"; given the connotations of the fig tree, it marks the courtyard of the "brown women" in "Andenken" as the place of his own undoing.

In the first two versions of the strophe, those who, like "great Ajax," died by their own hand, the "many sad ones of wild spirit," are set apart from those who died in battle, in the grip of their destiny. Since Hölderlin, however, considers both to be "divinely compelled," the third version retains only the terse statement that there died "many others as well." Hölderlin's commingling of references to both Sophocles's *Ajax* and Pindar's *Second Nemean Ode* (pointed out first by Szondi)[39] further effaces any demarcation between exalted heroic passion and destructive madness. As Haverkamp writes:

> The form of the tragic monologue, and the scheme of heroic eulogy are "mixed" in such a way that Pindar's scheme . . . is fulfilled and surpassed by the Sophoclean monologue. Pindar writes "and truly she, the Salamis [the "unmoved Salamis" of "Mnemosyne"] was able to rear a man deadly in battle . . ." In Sophocles, however, this same man, calling to his distant Salamis, succumbs to madness and ends in suicide.[40]

In a radicalization without earlier precedent, the third version passes from the death of the legendary heroes and of the unremembered "many others" to the ruin of Mnemosyne's city, Eleutherai ("Elevthera") and to the death of Mnemosyne herself. The slopes of the Kithairon on which, as Hölderlin notes, the ruined city lay were a locus of the Bacchic cult and of tragic myth, and were thus exposed to the heavenly fire. The city's name connotes *eleutheria*, freedom, which Hölderlin assimilated to the boundless; but, at the same time, it is the symbol of free poetic commemoration that lies in ruins. As Hölderlin notes in the ode *Stimme des Volkes*, the passion for the boundless and thus for death (*Todeslust*) seizes not only individuals but entire peoples and their "heroic cities."

When God "removed his cloak," which had shielded mortals from the unbearable splendor of his countenance, he laid waste the order of the city. The "evening-like" (*das Abendliche*), which is a figure of death and, in particular, of the occidental (*abendländischen*) obliteration of ancient Greece, then "severed the locks" of Mnemosyne. In accordance with ancient belief, she was thus consecrated to death.[41] The question, "Aber was ist diss?," is then at last answered in the concluding verses: the "heavenly ones" are "unwilling" and refuse their gift to one who cannot, first of all, preserve himself by "pulling together" his soul. The gift of poetic commemoration thus eludes one who cannot resolutely oppose what Hölderlin likes to call "the steadfast letter" (den vesten Buchstab) to the unwritten wilderness. However, just as the heroes of Greek antiquity died "divinely compelled," the poet also fails under ineluctable compulsion; for all his insight, he too is compelled: he "must nevertheless" ("aber er muss doch"), being unable to restrain his excessive passion.

The terse and enigmatic statement that concludes the poem, " . . . dem / Gleich fehlet die Trauer,"[42] is largely glossed over by commentators or interpreted as the poet's rejection of sentimentality and nostalgia.[43] The statement has its grammatical analogue in Hölderlin's "Der Einzige" (I, v.103); the parallel suggests the somewhat strained interpretation that mourning fails or errs like the one who cannot keep his soul together. Since the verb fehlet, however, indicates lack rather than erring, a more literal reading affirms that poetic mourning is lacking, in keeping with the lack of a poet who can receive the gift of the heavenly ones. Haverkamp thus concludes that "mourning's error is grounded in the absence of mourning and consists of nothing but its lack."[44]

The two interpretations are not necessarily incompatible: if sorrow, like the wild spirit of heroic excess, cannot gather itself into the living unity of poetic commemoration (thus erring or going astray), then mourning, in its tragic form (tragedy as Trauerspiel), as the poetic maintenance of measure and differentiation, will fail and be lacking. There will be no resistance to what Nietzsche called the Dionysian principle, the terrible unification that effaces human identity and the order of the polis. With respect to "Andenken," what is called into question is the poet's rapt attentiveness to "mortal thoughts," his access to the past through spontaneous commemoration, his solitary return to the source, and, above all, his ability to institute "that which abides." A salutary epochal transition issuing in a new world-configuration then becomes impossible; decline (Untergang) and transition (Übergang) are rendered disjunct; transformative energies are drawn into a catastrophic vortex. Given that, for Hölderlin, in contradistinction to Hegel, the question of tragedy is not historically surpassed but remains the central and living religious-historical question,[45] the bearing of such a disaster is momentous.

III

Heidegger remains unwilling—even in the face of Germany's "politics" of annihilation—to acknowledge disruption, failure, or catastrophe. This resistance is what holds him back from a reading of "Mnemosyne" (the sort of reading that, in deconstructionist parlance, reads the text's unreadability) and installs him instead on its threshold. In its commitment to maintaining, even *in extremis*, an ambiguity between danger and saving that derives from the "polemic" structure of *alētheia*, Heidegger's thought remains closer to Hegel's conception of tragic reconciliation (which, as Düsing remarks, safeguards "the contemplation of tragedy . . . against a plunge into despair")[46] than to Hölderlin's espousal of risk. His thought of Difference as *polemos* and differential "entrustment" or conciliation is not Hölderlin's thought of "boundless separation." For this reason, his commemorative retrieval of ancient Greece is not menaced by the risk of impassioned identification, in which the speculative structure of tragedy is collapsed; rather, he commemorates by projecting the *essential* "unsaid" of Greek saying onto the horizons of the future.

In the "Remarks on Oedipus," Hölderlin analyzes tragic structure in terms of "divine faithlessness," which marks the moment when time "turns categorically" (FA 16, 258).[47] At this point, man's path reverses itself, because, in the extremity of pain and suffering, he is deprived of temporal continuity (in particular, of the anticipated future) and is thrown back upon "the empty conditions of time and space" experienced as the sheer moment without issue. In Levinasian terms, this might be described as the experience of being riveted to the solitude of existing without possible retreat.[48] Divinity, on the other hand, turns away from man in faithlessness by manifesting itself as "nothing but time." This radical temporality negates *archē* and *telos* and the possibility of achieving meaning in history. For Hölderlin, however, such abandonment is "holy" rather than destructive, for, precisely "in the all-forgetting form of faithlessness," it preserves "the memory of the heavenly ones." Catharsis as tragic separation maintains commemoration and restores the very possibility of thought. Lacoue-Labarthe states the point succinctly:

> And we must note that this moment, which is a moment of "forgetting"—of the god and of oneself—is the condition of possibility of all memory and of all (faithless) fidelity, that is to say, the possibility of all thought.[49]

Hölderlin himself, interestingly enough, thematizes this origination of memory and thought in tragic faithlessness as *writing* (deprived of its secondariness to speech as an origin), by citing, in altered form, a quotation attributed by Sattler to Suidas: τῆς φυσέως λϱαμματεύς ἠν τὸν κάλαμον ἀποβϱέχων εὔνουν.[50] The obvious kinship of this thematization to the contemporary problematic of writing as *archē*-trace cannot, however, be further developed here.

Allemann has pointed out that Hölderlin's mature thought of radical temporalization already announces itself in the Rhine hymn, in that the "destinal balance" achieved prevails for a transient "while" (v.183). This Hölderlinian emphasis, Allemann notes, enters Heidegger's articulation "in a concealed way," such that "whiling" becomes the time-character of manifestation.[51] For Hölderlin, it is ultimately the thought of unstilled and discordant temporalization that sets in motion what Lacoue-Labarthe calls his unwilling deconstruction of the speculative matrix of tragedy.[52]

Although Heidegger's own understanding of temporalization (*Temporalität des Seins*) far surpasses the mere thought of finitude, and certainly at least prefigures the *archē*-trace, it does not accord with Hölderlin's treatment of the destinal or tragic moment as sheer "counter-rhythmic interruption," empty of all content and therefore refractory to (re)presentation. Heidegger's emphasis, even in his reading of Hölderlin's late poetry, is on "the infinite interconnection of the entire relationship" and on historicity as configuration rather than disfiguration. More importantly still, he does not countenance the possibility of a disaster that is bereft of saving power and that lies outside the sphere of tragedy and brings with it the failure of commemoration if not the erosion of language itself. Heidegger's unwillingness or inability to address the Shoah may be considered in this light, together with the fact that, on the rare occasions when he at least alludes to it, he submits it to the logic of technicity, which conjoins danger and saving.[53] Heidegger seems to have been incapable, furthermore, of acknowledging the opening to totalization in his own understanding of occidental history and in his rhetoric of spirit; for he considers all historical configuration to be differential, and spiritual "destinies," in particular, to be "polemic" in their very structure and thus refractory to totalizing moves.

If Mnemosyne's death and the failure of mourning constitute a disaster which destroys poetic commemoration, they do not, for all that, render impossible what Blanchot calls the writing of the disaster.[54] In this spirit, Edmond Jabès asserts that:

> To Adorno's statement that "After Auschwitz one can no longer write poetry," inviting a global questioning of our culture, I am tempted to answer: yes, one can. And furthermore, one has to. One has to write out of that break, out of that unceasingly revived wound.[55]

Such a writing out of rupture is, above all, that of Paul Celan. For Hölderlin himself, of course, the disaster took on a different configuration and called for a somewhat different response. This response, evident in the cryptic texts of the hymnic fragments and in the poetry of Hölderlin's madness, which lies beyond the failure of mourning, has been characterized as one of "humility," or "modesty."[56] Such "humility" can be interpreted along two lines: a transformation of language and of the hermeneutical function of poetry, and the exaltation, in Hölderlin's last poetry, of the simplest of earthly things in their sheer suchness and enigmatic simplicity.

It is one of the merits of Heidegger's reading of Hölderlin that he gives serious consideration to the work that lies beyond the failure of mourning. Allemann, indeed, argues that the trajectory of Heidegger's thinking led him, of its own momentum, into the unprotected extremity of engaging with a poetry that lies beyond the assurances of human meaning.[57] One needs to ask, however, what is the nature of this engagement.

What is utterly astonishing is that Heidegger reads the hymnic fragments—such as "Griechenland"—in exactly the same way he reads Hölderlin's great hymns, elegies, and other classical texts. This same reading is extended, furthermore, to Hölderlin's last poetry, down to the short poem, also titled "Griechenland," written in the year of the poet's death.[58] He refuses the passage through the failure of mourning that imperils the historically instituting and founding labors of poet and thinker, as well as what Hamlin calls "the self-reflective power of language, its capacity through utterance to know itself or to become conscious of its own meaning."[59] In keeping with this refusal, Heidegger shows no awareness of the hermeneutical problems posed by the virtual unreadability of a text like "Griechenland" (the hymnic fragment), given not only its cryptic articulation but the palimpsest character and literal indecipherability of the manuscript, for which no authoritative reading can be critically established.[60]

Heidegger reads the text as a decipherable cryptogram to which the thinker, in dialogue with the poet, holds the key. Once this key is resorted to, the text's labyrinthine complexities disclose to him a coherent configuration in which the smallest detail can be "elucidated" and accounted for in retrospect. This "stupefying" (Hamlin's term) appropriation of a writing that repudiates totalization is, of course, what provoked Adorno's sharp critique and his insistence on fragmentation and "parataxis" as distinctive features of the Hölderlinian text.[61]

The constraints which govern Heidegger's reading are familiar: it is to bring about remembrance (*Gedächtnis*; cf. "Andenken," v.55), which is thought of as a transmutation (*Umstimmung*) of thinking "into a thinking experience of the midst of the limitless relationship: out of 'posure' (*Gestell*) as the self-dissembling coming-into-its-own (*Ereignis*) of the Fourfold" (GA 4, 153). Such a transmutation requires the advent of the spared "great beginning": the Orient of ancient Greece must rise in its withheld *essentiality* upon the Occidental horizon. Only thus can Europe free itself from the grip of technicity and become, in Valéry's phrase (cited by

Heidegger), "the precious part of the entire earth, the pearl of the sphere, the brain of a vast body."[62] Heidegger voices the conviction that the present "planetary-interstellar world-configuration is in its *essen*tial origin, of which it cannot divest itself, through and through European-Occidental-Greek." He seeks to temper his Eurocentrism by adding that only with such a change in thinking will the West be able to open itself "to the few other great beginnings which, through what is their own, belong into the sameness of the beginning of the limitless relationship . . ." (GA 4, 177). It is not clear whether, given that sameness, he regards them as having anything distinctive to contribute.

Within the structure of this geo-philosophy and geo-history, Hölderlin's poem ("Griechenland," as well as what Heidegger likes to call the single "unsaid" poem which is the source of a poet's work) supposedly allows those caught up in the crisis of technicity to *think* the refusal which keeps in abeyance the enabling midst of the Fourfold, "pure destiny itself," and to anticipate the advent, in difference, of the spared beginning. Heidegger's engagement with Hölderlin's late poetry thus circumvents the rupture which is the death of Mnemosyne and the failure of mourning, as well as the "other" writing and thinking released by this rupture.

To explore the character of this other writing, with respect to Hölderlin, requires a study of texts such as "Griechenland" along lines opened up not by Heidegger but by interpreters such as Renate Böschenstein-Schäfer, who studies the undoing of the classical sign-structure, the elision of hierarchization (and thus of representation), and "cognitive withdrawal" in this writing, together with the changed configuration of "the world as language."[63] This other writing, furthermore, must be interrogated as to its repudiation of the politics of domination and totalization.

The *other* aspect of such a writing which must be thematized is its conjunction of intellectual severity not only with releasement but with what Hölderlin likes to call "love" or "tenderness":

> . . . Wo darauf
> Tönend wie des Kalbs Haut
> Die Erde, von Verwüstungen her, Versuchungen der Heiligen
> Denn anfangs bildet das Werk sich
> Grossen Gesetzen nachgehet, die Wissenschaft
> Und Zärtlichkeit und den Himmel breit lauter Hülle nachher
> Erscheinend singen Gesangeswolken.
> Denn fest ist der Erde
> Nabel. Gefangen nemlich in Ufern von Gras sind
> Die Elammen und die allgemeinen

Elemente. Lauter Besinnung aber oben lebt der Aether. Aber
   silbern
An reinen Tagen
Ist das Licht. Als Zeichen der Liebe
Veilchenblau die Erde.[64]

Heidegger reads "tenderness" as a trope of the bridal feast which the poet speaks of in the second version; and, with characteristic concern for the hidden logic of every detail, he adds that, through the red of the earth (taking this color characterization from Hölderlin's "Der Vatikan"), the blueness of the sky, seen from an earthly perspective, takes on a violet hue (GA 4, 173).

For Hölderlin, however, it is not the sky but the earth itself which, having withstood storms and devastation, now follows "great laws" and which appears, whatever its cosmic insignificance (wherein it differs from Heidegger's Europe), as a token of love, colored in the intense hue of the equally insignificant violet. (The violet in its conjunction with love may be read, parenthetically, as an allusion to Sappho.) In contrast to the uproar of the captive elements and "ancient laws of the earth" in "Mnemosyne," the elements and the searing flames are now held captive by simple "shores of grass." Since the violet earth, in the pure light, lies centered and firm, "clouds of song" celebrate both knowledge and tenderness and the radiance of "the sky vast of pure raiment." There is here no Heideggerian projection of the future out of the withheld past, nor any critique of the present; rather, the poem (which is self-reflective) affirms the power of art to create an order of pure differentiation within which what is given here and now can in every way be attended to. Whatever may be its conventional insignificance, it can then show itself in its *phainesthai*, in the inexhaustibility of its sheer suchness. To seek the enigma, as Heidegger does, in the problematic and erased position of origin is to fail to find *in and as what* now presences or is manifest.

6

◆

A Missed Interlocution: Heidegger and Celan

... Blumen fangen
Vor Thoren der Stadt an, auf geebneten Wegen unbegünstigt
Gleich Krystallen in der Wüste wachsend des Meers.

Hölderlin, "Griechenland"

... Flowers begin
before the city gates, on trodden paths unfavored
like crystals growing in the desert of the sea.

Although Heidegger was certainly no stranger to Paul Celan's poetry and is, indeed, attested to have been in correspondence with the poet beginning in 1957 (some ten years before the first or their two meetings, which took place in July 1967),[1] there is no trace of Celan in the corpus of Heidegger's writings on poetry and poetics. His strange silence concerning Celan uncannily recalls his stubborn silence concerning the Holocaust.[2]

Quite apart from the circumstance that, in the decade between the beginning of their correspondence and the first meeting Celan was emerging and coming to be recognized as one of the foremost poets of the German language, Heidegger's silence is astonishing for several reasons. Celan, first of all, is the contemporary poet who consciously carries forward the legacy of Hölderlin, indeed, also of Trakl and Rilke; and, as Sieghild Bogumil observes, this is "precisely that tradition in which Heidegger saw the poetic word, in its essence, coming to appearance in a privileged way."[3] Secondly, the exigencies of Heidegger's own thought on language and its role in the happening of manifestation ought to have impelled him to seek interlocution with a poet who problematizes what Werner Hamacher and Evelyn Hünneke have called, with different emphases, the fissioning im/partment of language and the realization of the real in the medium of poetry.[4]

Celan questions, in particular, the possibilities of meaning, commemoration, and communion still open to a language which has been despoiled by history. This consideration leads to a third point: if Heidegger's interlocution with Hölderlin constituted, at least in part, an encrypted "confrontation" with National Socialism,[5] how could he fail eventually to extend this interlocution to Celan, who not only writes out of the Jewish experience of persecution but who also speaks to the condition of "survival" as a contemporary condition not limited to the Jews.[6] Lastly, Celan's poetry not only problematizes itself in a manner that responds to what Heidegger calls a "destitute time" but it is already in responsive relationship to Heidegger's thought; for Celan (unlike those who today advocate a dismissal of Heidegger) was an assiduous reader of Heidegger's works who often echoes and transforms Heideggerian thought-structures.

How is one to understand Heidegger's sustained silence and the failure of interlocution? Circumstantial considerations do not suffice. However, Celan's poem "Todtnauberg," which commemorates the 1967 meeting, can offer here at least a preliminary "situation":

Todtnauberg

Arnika, Augentrost, der
Trunk aus dem Brunnen mit dem
Sternwürfel drauf,
in der
Hütte,
die in das Buch
—wessen Namen nahms auf
vor dem meinen?—,
die in dies Buch
geschriebene Zeile von
einer Hoffnung, heute,
auf eines Denkenden
kommendes
Wort
im Herzen,
Waldwasen, uneingeebnet,
Orchis und Orchis, einzeln.
Krudes, später, im Fahren,
deutlich,
der uns fährt, der Mensch,
der's mit anhört,
die halb-

> beschrittenen Knüppel-
> pfade im Hochmoor,
> Feuchtes,
> viel.[7]

The poem evokes the thinker's retreat in a work-enabling rural simplicity and solitude, as he himself experienced it: the plain homestead, fountain and stars, mountain flowers, the book, the moor. Celan, indeed, allows the landscape to come into discontinuous presencing in a manner which echoes Heidegger's own relationship to it:

> Strictly speaking, I never observe the landscape. I experience its hourly changes, day and night, in the great goings and comings of the seasons . . . the course of the work remains embedded in what happens in the region.[8]

However, the tranquility of this agrarian-intellectual idyll is menaced, in the poem, from the outset by the intrusion of history not only upon nature but into the very articulation of language, and thus into the modalities of manifestation. The casting (*Würfel/werfen*) of the star-die upon the water calls to mind the star of David as the symbol of "the youngest outcasting"; the homestead is a shack which recalls camp barracks; the book in which the survivor inscribes his name (as a place-holder for the untold effaced names) is not a book of life but one which may conceal the names of those who were in complicity with murder. The life-sustaining and cleansing water of the fountain figures in what Bogumil calls "an isotopy of water" (perhaps, rather, a heterotopy and a tropology of transformation, in contrast to Heidegger's habitual isotopy of soil and ground) which conjoins life-giving and healing (*Augentrost* is "eyebright," literally the "consolation of the eyes") with the implication of weeping and a disabling pervasiveness of "the moist." The last figure, placed at the end of the poem, responds to the initial suggestion of wounding (arnica is a medicinal herb) and tears and may also indicate the displacement of genuine conversation and communion from "the heart" by sentimental effusion. Finally, the uncommon term *Waldwasen* (linked to burial practices) for "woodland swards" may, as Pöggeler suggests, recall that (whereas no one normally expects woodlands to be levelled) the naturally rolling ground around Auschwitz was levelled with the ashes of the dead.[9] Since there is no landscape, whether of nature or thought, that is not inscribed by history, the "woodpaths" (*Holz*-wege) of the thinker's questioning have become "rod-paths," which not only connote violence and discontinuity but also can be taken only halfway, so that even their bearing into what Heidegger calls "the wayless" (*das Unwegsame*) is aborted.

Whereas Heidegger writes that his mountain solitude "has the peculiar and original power of not isolating us but of projecting our whole existence out into the vast nearness of the presence (*Wesen*) of all beings,"[10] Celan articulates fragmentation and isolation: "orchid and orchid" stand next to one another in their singularity, speech becomes significant only as an uncouth "crudeness" that dawns on one after the hearing; and the hope, growing "in the heart," for a "coming / word" which would spring from the same place remains unfulfilled. Celan's very language—that of the poet who, out of the historical destitution of *today* (rather than a destitution that, as Heidegger holds, has not yet truly come to experience),[11] seeks out the thinker—is fragmented and halting. It holds itself, nevertheless, in what Celan called the *topos* of encounter, thus also holding itself out not to a mythicized figure but to the living person of the Other, the thinker as one caught up in and responsive to the same historical configuration. However, instead of a possible renewal of human community as what, for Blanchot, is "the unavowable community" of survivors,[12] let alone an attentive "sharing" in "the presencing of all beings," interlocution is at best half-fulfilled in displacement. The one who is "with it" (in a genuine *Mitsein*) by silent and thoughtful listening is the anonymous "man," whose undistinguished and technological vocation is driving.

As Bogumil observes, Heidegger could relate to the poet only as one who "quietly perseveres in the eternal response of language"; and language itself, as the "unbinding bond" that engages man not in historical human community but to receive and respond to "the tidings" of the Differing,[13] remained, for him, essentially unbroken. These considerations concerning historicity, language, and community serve to circumscribe a *topos* of rupture, the topography of which needs to be more specifically explored.

I

Heidegger marks the *essential* place (*Ort*) of a poet's poetic saying as a point of convergence "at the tip of the spear," which indicates the "highest and utmost" inner necessity of the saying. This gathering *in extremis* thus responds to or converges with the hidden source or origin of the saying, which, for Heidegger, remains dislocated into the "unsaid." He insists that the "wave" of poetic saying, in its rhythmic surging forth, does not abandon the source but rather "lets all the movement (*Bewegen*, way-making) of the saying flow back into the ever more concealed origin."[14] The origin and gathering point concealed in the "unsaid" becomes the locus of the interlocution between poet and thinker; and the thinker's "severity" is called upon to "establish" it and render it firm. To enter into interlocution, the thinker must set into play the hermeneutic reciprocity between "situating" (*erörtern*) and elucidating (*erläutern*), thus making possible the release of meaning at the crux of their chiasm. Heidegger's interpretive approach is governed throughout by the project of and search for differential unification, and by the need to construe such unification as post-metaphysical and thus post-Hegelian, which is to say, as no longer functioning within the "closed economy" (Bataille's term) of the self-unfolding of the Absolute. Heidegger reads both Hölderlin and Trakl out of this search for a post-metaphysical and differential unification, which remains "spiritual" precisely in that spirit unifies "polemically" and thus contains within itself the power of transition (*Übergang*) and transformation.

In a late poem that forms part of the posthumous collection *Zeitgehöft*, Celan articulates his own relationship to Hölderlin:

> Ich trink Wein aus zwei Gläsern
> und zackere an
> der Königszäsur
> wie Jener
> am Pindar,
>
> Gott gibt die Stimmgabel ab
> als einer der kleinen
> Gerechten,
>
> aus der Lostrommel fällt
> unser Deut.[15]

Hölderlin's notion of the *caesura*, formulated on the basis of his work on Pindar and Greek tragedy, is that of a "counter-rhythmic interruption" by the "pure word," which, at the height of tragic transport, allows representation (*Vorstellung*) to show itself as such, in its law:

> Thereby the sequence of the calculation, as well as the rhythm are divided; and [the sequence], in its two halves, is interrelated in such a manner that they, as carrying equal weight, appear.[16]

The division effected by the *caesura* resembles the structure of the equipollence of Pyrrhonian skepticism, in that it frustrates both (dialectical) unification and decisive orientation. Its function, for Hölderlin, is cathartic; it "purifies" the tendency to "limitless unification" by "limitless separation" (FA 14, 257). In sharp contrast to the articulations of convergence in Heidegger's poetics, the Hölderlinian *caesura* is a marker of divergence. The gap of the *caesura* falls outside of philosophical economies (for which reason, precisely, it is able to let representation show itself as such). Hölderlin's own laborious "zig-zagging" or "oscillating" (the verb *zackern* indicates that the "tip" is reached only to be abandoned again and dislocated in repetition)[17] circumscription of the Greeks cannot accomplish a Heideggerian *essentializing* retrieval, but yields heterology.

The division of the *caesura* is intensified in Celan's explicit negation of any unified source of poetic inspiration—the "draught of vintage" of traceable provenance. The labor of the poet who oscillates between "two glasses" carries even a connotation of sterility and of the ridiculous. Since his own bond to Hölderlin is, paradoxically, one of disseverance (which is not, of course, a simple lack of connection), his displacement from the classical Western tradition is raised, as it were, to the second power. This may be interpreted as meaning that the duality that governed Hölderlin's relationship to the Greeks has given way to a dissemination or dehiscence (let the reader choose between Derrida and Merleau-Ponty) in multiplicity.

Hölderlin's God, furthermore, has given over the "tuning fork" (and thus the possibility of an Heideggerian *Umstimmung* of presencing) to the inconspicuous "small just ones" of Jewish mysticism.[18] Poetic meaning, which has become communalized and even vulgarized as *unser Deut*, no longer allows itself to be col-lected at the acme of convergence prepared for by the craftsmanship (*Handwerk*) of Heideggerian poetizing and thinking. It falls, instead, as chance may dictate, out of the spinning drum that allots destiny—not because the poet is careless but because the possibility of a convergence in the "unsaid" has become superseded. What supersedes it is what Celan in "A la pointe acérée" (another poem thematizing the tip of the spear) calls "things unwritten," which, in the cataclysms of recent history, have "hardened into language."[19] The consequent sclerosis of language no longer allows for the supple movements of surging forth and recollective confluence, nor yet for the poet's or the thinker's prescriptive col-lecting of meaning.

The configuration of Celan's complex articulation of the thematic of *lesen* (which involves reading, col-lecting, se-lecting, *legein*, laying-out, and letting-lie-before) may be indicated with reference to "A la pointe acérée." In virtue of an historical upheaval, the hidden things of the earth, "the ores, the crystals,/ the geodes," are cast out and lie bare, "crosswise," shamelessly exposed in disorder. While they do not allow for an Heideggerian reading that is "drawn and, at the same time, sustained by the fundamental trait of sheltering,"[20] their exposure nevertheless "lays bare a sky." This is not the secure sky of Heidegger's Fourfold but one which, in the "turning of the breath" (*Atemwende*, which takes the place of *caesura*), may yawn as an abyss before one's feet.[21] There is, for Celan, no univocal reading either of the symbols of history (the "killed / chalk-star") or of its orientation. No saying and col-lecting can therefore prepare for an Heideggerian turning "from out of the abyss." Reading, nevertheless, remains a necessity: it traces its *Holzwege* as "ways thither" (to the site of the death camp) in the quiet of the "woodland hour," and questions, with the searching touch of "finger-thoughts" (rather than with the detached "eye"), what is "unrepeatable" and thus refractory to language.

For Heidegger, the disclosive power of poetic language, together with its ability to open up the dimension of human dwelling and to give it a layout (*Einrichtung*), remains *essentially* unaffected by history. For this reason, he can affirm that the thinkers and poets of the tradition that, as Alan Udoff puts it, "may be traced back to the ruins of Troy and forward to a castle in Muzot,"[22] say "the same" in historical difference. This dimension of dwelling is, to be sure, a Western one; for Heidegger surmises that, if language is the house of Being, "we Europeans dwell presumably in a house quite different from that of East Asian humanity," with scarcely any possibility of a conversation "from house to house" (GA 12, 85).

The thought of poetry as the establishment of human dwelling is not Heidegger's alone but is characteristic of modernity. Udoff, in the cited study, explores its articulation in Hegel and Rilke, noting that, for Celan, the point of the metaphorics of home, dwelling, root, or ground is to describe the nature of the self in a disruption for which the only oblique analogue in the tradition of modernity is found in Hölderlin's late poetics. This disruption is due not to the sheer massiveness of evil but to certain structural aspects of the Shoah that are theoretically explored by Udoff and by Lacoue-Labarthe: a systematic destruction of the resources and integrity of the self as the source of *poiēsis*, the instilling, in the survivors, of "the shame of Being" (which negates the Heideggerian "care-taking of Being"), and finally, what Lacoue-Labarthe calls "the useless residue (*le déchet*) of the Western idea of art, that is to say, of *technē*."[23]

Celan's poetry and poetics, which finds itself dislocated to the zero point of this devastation, strives nevertheless to reconfigure itself in response to the urgency of another mandate. How Celan conceived of the possibility and mandate of "poetry after Auschwitz" (to echo Adorno) will be explored here through a reading of his poem "Engführung" ("Stretta") which forms part of the 1959 collection *Sprachgitter*, and of which Szondi has performed a pathbreaking exegesis.[24]

II

Although the present study, in view of its interrogative focus, will not attempt a full exegesis of "Engführung," it will move sequentially through the poem's nine sections. These sections (arranged in a menorah-like configuration of 4 + 1 + 4) are interlinked by the reprise of textual fragments in a manner that contributes to the suggestion of the musical form of the *stretta*. The latter is the third and last part of the structure of the fugue, in which, according to Szondi's citation from *Der grosse Brockhaus*, "the rapid succession of the canonic entry themes of the different voices produces an especially intense, interlaced contrapuntal pattern." Although this interlacing of voices in the poem creates a certain poetic "constancy,"[25] or what Heidegger calls a sameness without identity, reflecting both compositional "severity" and a sustained focus of concern, Celan's plurivocity repudiates the accord of the "higher univocity" which Heidegger discerns in Trakl (GA 12, 71). It remains, rather, irresolubly "in the straits," leading Szondi to advocate "an at least partial avoidance of discursive speech," an avoidance of closure, and attentiveness to textual function rather than meaning on the interpreter's part.[26] Celan's reprise of the Heideggerian conceit of the fugue transposes both this conceit and the traditional musical form (to the structure of which Celan is more attentive than Heidegger) into the field of a new textuality.

Bogumil, reflecting on the tension, in both Hölderlin and Celan, between compositional severity and a transgression of the historico-poetic constraints of language, points out that Hölderlin could solicit (using this word here in its Derridean sense) such constraints only from within a poetic and rhetorical canon, whereas Celan moved in the space of a new structural and deconstructive freedom.[27] This difference between the two poets is fundamentally what allows Heidegger to engage in interlocution with one but not the other; for Hölderlin's poetry, in its recognition of formal canons, is not refractory to a gathering into univocity which deflects its transgressive power. Much the same can be said of Trakl, whose espousal of folksong and religious motifs creates a semblance of "hidden harmony"; but Celan's poetic diction implacably frustrates unifying and crypto-eschatological moves. It is certainly significant that Heidegger's only contemporary interlocutor is Stefan George, who died in 1934, and that the "pulverized poem," the *parole en archipel*, even of René Char, with whom the philosopher maintained a personal friendship, did not enter into the interlocutory texts.

The first section of "Engführung" reads as follows:

> Verbracht ins
> Gelände
> mit der untrüglichen Spur:

> Gras, auseinandergeschrieben. Die Steine, weiss,
> mit den Schatten der Halme:
> Lies nicht mehr—schau!
> Schau nicht mehr—geh!

> Geh, deine Stunde
> hat keine Schwestern, du bist—
> bist zuhause. Ein Rad, langsam,
> rollt aus sich selber, die Speichen
> klettern auf schwärzlichem Feld, die Nacht

> braucht keine Sterne, nirgends
> fragt es nach dir.[28]

The terrain into which one/it finds one/itself deported is not a landscape of human dwelling but a terrain of the trace, a textual landscape. The line break (*Gelände / mit*) does not allow for an interpretive decision as to whether it is the terrain alone that bears the undeceiving trace or whether the one/what-is-deported likewise remains marked by it. Szondi, after following a somewhat different line of interpretation, remarks that it becomes impossible to distinguish between the reader and what is read or read about.[29]

The second verse ends in a colon and opens, therefore, upon a descriptive specification of terrain and trace. In this blank terrain, what becomes trace or reveals the trace is "grass, written asunder"—grass, which, as Szondi notes, can also be "read" as having been deported but which is undeceiving in its inability to restore rural innocence. In being written asunder, the grass traces its shadow-writing on the white stones (note that the initial "with" of the fourth verse creates a parallel to the second).

Like the writing upon Trakl's "old stone" (which is understood by Heidegger as hardened pain; GA 12, 59), this lithic shadow-writing inscribes itself in the mode of direct address; but the implied "you" which is here addressed is singular and familiar, rather than plural and impersonal, and it is given not a promise but a command. It is enjoined no longer to "read" and decipher but to "look" upon what is inescapable, yet also (in the rhetoric of *correctio*, which Szondi points out throughout the poem) no longer to "look" with specular detachment but to "go" into the textual terrain that does not allow itself to be read.

This imperative is not the Hölderlinian imperative to go and greet, so as to achieve recollection in a sisterly hour; for the hour or time-space into which it drives the one who is addressed is cut off and unrepeatable. If what is commanded to go forth is (also) the poem (Celan's poetry throughout is self-reflective and self-problematizing), the time-space of origin in which it is at home is a point of effacement.

As concerns home and the "wheel" (a traditional symbol of time and the seasons), it is instructive to read Celan's text against a passage from Heidegger's essay on Hölderlin's elegy "Heimkunft / An die Verwandten":

> "The house" means here the space which is, in each case, laid out (*eingeräumt*) for human beings, wherein alone they can be "at home" and thus in the propriety (*im Eigenen*) of their destiny. This space is the gift of the inviolate earth ... "The year" here lays out (*räumt ein*) the times known to us as the seasons ... "The year" offers its greeting in the play of light. (GA 4, 17)

Celan's poem, by contrast, is at home in and must go forth from a destinal time/space of refusal; instead of laying out the course of times and seasons, it rolls blindly "out of itself," its climbing spokes revealing and inscribing, instead of a play of light, a "blackish field." Whereas Heidegger's poet and thinker contemplate destiny's stellar course (*Sternengang*), the night here is devoid of and needs no orienting stars; nowhere is the poet/poem of this destitute time being asked for.

> Nirgends
> fragt es nach dir—
> Der Ort, wo sie lagen, er hat
> einen Namen—er hat
> keinen. Sie lagen nicht dort. Etwas
> lag zwischen ihnen. Sie
> sahn nicht hindurch.
> Sahn nicht, nein,
> redeten von
> Worten. Keines
> erwachte, der
> Schlaf
> kam über sie.[30]

The first reprise is a simple echo: the fact that the poem is nowhere asked for appears to be linked to a failure of poetic naming, an erasure of name and place. *Correctio* functions here, not in the service of precise determination but of indeterminability and ellipsis. Both the representational character and the disclosive power of language are problematized in a manner that, as Allemann notes (without specific reference to "Engführung"), unsettles the reciprocity between word and thing. He understands this reciprocity as comprising not only the representational model of language but also what George indicates by insisting that "no thing can be where the word fails."[31] If one recalls here Heidegger's commentary to the effect that the word which fails to come to language is the word for the *essencing* of language, or for the way in which "saying and Being, word and thing belong together in a concealed, barely considered, and unthinkable manner" (making for the *essential* relationship between poetizing and thinking),[32] one recognizes the bearing of Celan's negations and questioning: those who lay/did not lie in a nameless place in the textual terrain of the trace experienced language as opacity rather than as granting disclosure; their speaking was "of words" only; not one among them (the words as well as the speakers) awoke to the power of the *logos*; what "came" to them was not the advent of the concealed promise of the past from out of the future, but sleep, which closes off the temporal ecstases.

> Kam, kam, Nirgends
> fragt es—
> Ich bins, ich,
> ich lag zwischen euch, ich war
> offen, war
> hörbar, ich tickte euch zu, euer Atem
> gehorchte, ich
> bin es noch immer, ihr
> schlaft ja.[33]

Among the echoes of sleep's coming and of being nowhere asked for, another coming announces itself with the insistency of repetition and the directness of the first person singular and the present tense—a coming whose essence, as Szondi puts it, is arrival. Yet that which, in its coming, reveals its openness and the constancy of its Being is what already "lay between you," unrecognized but sustaining temporality and interconnection.

Szondi points out that *ticken*, a verb which now signifies the ticking of clock time, earlier carried also the meaning of "to touch with the fingertips."[34] Even in sleep and oblivion, this "ticking" remained audible, and its awakening touch was felt; for the breath (life-force, spirit, speaking) of the sleepers responded. Now, however, the sleepers seem to lie lifeless, beyond recall, and debarred from the opening.

> Bin es noch immer—
> Jahre.
> Jahre, Jahre, ein Finger
> tastet hinab und hinan, tastet
> umher:
> Nahtstellen, fühlbar, hier
> klafft es weit auseinander, hier
> wuchs es wieder zusammen—wer
> deckte es zu?[35]

The call which asserts itself in constancy throughout years of darkness is a call to remembrance, to bear witness. The searching touch of a (synecdochic) finger responds, at last, to this *zuticken* by its own searching touch, feeling its way into a terrain of memory and exploring the wound-gaping, the scar-tissue, that which lay covered over and covered up in an ambiguous gesture both compassionate and concealing.

> Deckte es
> zu—wer?
> Kam, kam.
> Kam ein Wort, kam,

kam durch die Nacht,
wollt' leuchten, wollt' leuchten.

Asche.
Asche, Asche.
Nacht.
Nacht-und-Nacht.—Zum
Aug geh, zum feuchten.[36]

What "came" irrepressibly, at last, was a "word" to dispel sleep, to penetrate the obscuration, to accomplish *phainesthai*, to render manifest what the searching finger discovered in the dark.

One must agree with Szondi that, in this fifth and central section (given the scheme of 4 + 1 + 4), a decisive turning-point is reached in the transition between the two strophes (and thus at the poem's exact center). The word, which in its coming sought to shine, is suffocated by ashes and by night closing in upon itself, which repudiates all illumination. The quest for remembrance and witness, however, which led from the present into the past, does not, "where the word fails," simply leave the present as it was before. Rather, in a new response to the initial commands to "look" and "go," it is now redirected to bear witness in a new way, by going to the moist eye, which, in its weeping, is incapable of luminosity and panoramic vision.

Once it is admitted that, as Gadamer puts it, "the postulate of harmony, which we have so far kept intact as an assured expectation of meaning in every encountered obscuration of meaning, has withdrawn itself,"[37] the poetic word is released from the task of illumination. In being sent into the depths of mourning, it abandons the fiery element (illumination, *phainesthai*) and enters into the dark turbulence of the primal waters, into storms and whirlwinds (*Orkane*) reminiscent of Leonardo's obsessive drawings of the Deluge. Since the word here disseminates itself with bewildering prolixity, the sixth section of "Engführung" is by far the longest and will be discussed in two parts:

[6.1]   Zum
                    Aug geh,
                        zum feuchten—

Orkane.
Orkane, von je,
Partikelgestöber, das andre,
du
weissts ja, wir
lasens im Buche, war
Meinung.

War, war
Meinung. Wie
fassten wir uns
an—an mit
diesen
Händen?

Es stand auch geschrieben, dass.
Wo? Wir
taten ein Schweigen darüber,
giftgestillt, gross,
ein
grünes
Schweigen, ein Kelchblatt, es
hing ein Gedanke an Pflanzliches dran—
grün, ja,
hing, ja,
unter hämischem
Himmel.

An, ja,
Pflanzliches.[38]

What is unleashed as the word issues out of mourning is a fissioning disarticulation of language, a textuality devoid of what Philippe Forget calls an original donation of sense.[39] In sharp contrast to Heidegger's understanding of poetic articulation as opening up ways to language, which would reveal its "*forma*, the *Gestalt* of the fitting-together, wherein the *essencing* of language which rests within *Ereignis* opens up ways,"[40] Celan here denies form, *essencing*, the fit or order of any cosmos, and the "ways" of disclosure and relatedness as sheer imputation (*Meinung*)—the sort of thing one encounters "in the book." Although a "you" is now introduced and poignantly addressed, allowing for the constitution of a "we," the person of the other and the possibility of communion are at once problematized as belonging to the structure of imputation.

The "we" of the third strophe indicates no community but rather the speaker's implication in a cultural work of dissembling and silencing. What this silencing and concealing refused to recognize was the terror of the nihilistic vision—albeit such terror perhaps was already announced in "the writ." The "poison-stilled" silencing calls to mind such Heideggerian tropes as the resounding of stillness, the stilling of pain (which transmutes it into "flaming regard"), or the stilling of man's unprotectedness. More importantly, Celan's thematic of the "green" and "plantlike" can be read as alluding to the Heideggerian interpretation of *physis* as a word for Being, for the very happening of manifestation, to the mythology of soil and rooted-ness, and to an organicist conception of the spiritual. All of these are compelling cultural and intellectual constructs, from which the speaker does not entirely dissociate himself but which are seen as forms of denial:

[6.2]   Ja.
          Orkane, Par-
          tikelgestöber, es blieb
          Zeit, blieb,
          es beim Stein zu versuchen—er
          war gastlich, er
          fiel nicht ins Wort. Wie
          gut wir es hatten.

          Körnig,
          körnig und faserig. Stengelig,
          dicht:
          traubig und strahlig; nierig,
          plattig und
          klumpig; locker, ver-
          ästelt—: er, es
          fiel nicht ins Wort, es
          sprach,
          sprach gerne zu trockenen Augen, eh es sie schloss.

          Sprach, sprach.
          War, war.

          Wir
          liessen nicht locker, standen
          inmitten, ein
          Porenbau, und
          es kam.

          Kam auf uns zu, kam
          hindurch, flickte
          unsichtbar, flickte
          an der letzten Membran,
          und
          die Welt, ein Tausendkristall,
          schoss an, schoss an.[41]

In the face of the terrifying vision, one realizes that the path which leads to the moist eye is a path without issue. There remains only "time"—the whirl, rush, and fissioning of particles, or what Werner Hamacher calls the fissioning im/partment of language.[42] The only way left now for the poetic word is "to try it out with the stone," which is emphatically not plantlike, and whose hardness, resistance, and opacity recall the earlier characterization of language as resistant to diaphanous presencing and to the effort to speak "through" or "across" it. It also presented itself, however, in a movement of *correctio* as open and "audible," in virtue of its very "ticking"; the poet moves now from the older sense of *ticken* as touching to ticking as sheer temporalization, the "ticking and ticking" of the "heart-stones" with their "indestructible clockwork," which Celan speaks of in "Und mit dem Buch aus Tarussa" (PC I, 287–291).

The speaking which leaves behind the moist, quasi-vegetative realm of remembrance and mourning, with its diachronic order, to achieve a synchronic crystallization, a spatialization, and solidification of time itself, may be interpreted as a Mallarméan pure poetry. This stone-speaking, as presented in the sixth strophe, consists of dyadic and triadic strings of adjectives (except for the singularized *dicht*, which can also be read as "poetize!"). These adjectives conjoin forms of both organic and inorganic nature without any growth principle, narrative order, or other evidence of historicity, without the metaphysical subject-predicate structure, and without subjectivity. The erasure of subjectivity is indicated by the shift from the gendered pronoun *er* (referring to the stone) to the ungrammatical neuter pronoun *es* in the seventh verse.

The price of continuing to speak and to affirm Being, of reconstituting the cosmos as a "thousand-crystal" out of poetic language, is a distancing from ordinary life involvements, which Celan likens, in his 1960 speech "Der Meridian," to the notion of art as a Medusa's head that turns living beings to stone (PC III, 192). The hospitable stone thus "did not interrupt": no mourning or metaphysical anguish disrupts the serenity of its speaking "to dry eyes" that, however, it eventually closes to the concerns of the times. Celan, in the seventh part of "Engführung," voices dissatisfaction with the crystalline purity and consummate formal play of pure poetry:

> Schoss an, schoss an.
>   Dann—
>
> Nächte, entmischt. Kreise,
> grün oder blau, rote
> Quadrate: die
> Welt setzt ihr Innerstes ein
> im Spiel mit den neuen

Stunden—Kreise,
rot oder schwarz, helle
Quadrate, kein
Flugschatten, kein
Messtisch, keine
Rauchseele steigt und spielt mit.[43]

The emphatic "then" in the reprise of the seventh section (the only new element introduced into a reprise) allows the crystalline world to appear that has, *per impossibile*, separated out the very darkness into a prism of spectral colors. The formal precision—without rigidity—of this world recalls Celan's characterization of the etchings, engravings, and lithographs of his wife, Gisèle Lestrange (which he acknowledged to be influential for his own work), as "crystallographic gestures" and "formulae rendered visible," which nevertheless allow for free play (*Spielraum*) and mystery.[44] That such play is no mere formalism is indicated by the fourth verse: the world which crystallized and displays its consummate formal structure now "pledges its inmost" in play with the "new hours." Not only is this play, then, intensely committed, but, as Gadamer has pointed out, pure poetry is not divorced from significance; for the very form of the poem depends on "the constantly shifting balance between sound and sense."[45] He notes that such poetry restores the ordinary word to its power of naming; it is perhaps this very power which releases the "new hours" (hours no longer "without sisters"), thus initiating a new temporal order.

What this crystalline cosmos excludes, however, is shadow and smoke, as well as any possibility of meaningful human encounter. One must agree with Szondi that the "flight's shadow," the "plane-table," and the "smoke-soul" are not and need not be univocally determinable (over-determination is characteristic of Celan's poetics); but some indications concerning these notions can be given. The absence of a flight's shadow brings home the ghostly insubstantiality of this poetic "mobile" of geometric simples and pure colors (and does so in paradox, since shadow is itself insubstantial), but it also sets off the importance of shadow-writing and trace-writing in the constitution of the poetic text. The plane-table, most importantly, allows for the charting of the meridians of interconnection (see chapter 7). Apart from its obvious reference to the crematoria and perhaps to Exodus 17.21–22, the smoke-soul also recalls certain Heraclitean fragments (B7, B98) concerning the need of the *psychē* to orient itself by smell in a smoke-world where vision fails. It is clear, however, that shadow and smoke are not to *displace* the lucid articulation of the world constituted out of language, but to *take part* in it, to "play along" (*mitspielen*).

>   Steigt und
>   spielt mit—
> In der Eulenflucht, beim
> versteinerten Aussatz,
> bei
> unsern geflohenen Händen, in
> der jüngsten Verwerfung,
> überm Kugelfang an
> der verschütteten Mauer:
>
> sichtbar, aufs
> neue: die
> Rillen, die
>
> Chöre, damals, die
> Psalmen. Ho, ho-
> sianna.
>
> Also
> stehen noch Tempel. Ein
> Stern
> hat wohl noch Licht.
> Nichts,
> nichts ist verloren.
>
> Ho-
> sianna.
>
> In der Eulenflucht, hier,
> die Gespräche, taggrau,
> der Grundwasserspuren.[46]

As the smoke-soul mounts and plays along (the reprise no longer negates this), one finds oneself returned to the terrain of the trace in the twilight hour of the owls' (not the gods') fleeing and flight. Fled also are "our hands" (with which "we / grasped each other"); and the crystal world has become the mineral realm of a petrified leprosy/outcasting (*versteinerter Aussatz* also brings into play Heidegger's "petrified pain" and the name Auschwitz). What becomes visible in and by the place/time of outcasting, however, is "above" the butts for target practice on the buried wall, surmounting the closure of the death camp. The narrow channels that show themselves anew are opened by "the / choirs at that time," the intoning of psalms, the stammering response to the brutal "ho, ho" as "ho-siannah," a cry for divine salvation and mercy.

Although, as Szondi writes, "the situational determinates replace and dissolve [or at least obscure] the pure, sharp, radiant elements" of the crystalline cosmos created out of language,[47] neither the poisoned silencing nor the terrifying nihilistic vision are reinstated. If, then, perhaps temples still stand or a (one) star still has light—if in this sense "nothing is lost"—this suffices for the repudiation of nothingness, of nihilistic negation (*Nichts*). Celan, however, is not voicing any simplistic acquiescence and hope. It is, after all, the frail word of the deported, condemned, and dying—the word spoken in extremity as prayer and cry, seeking an Other—which etched open the channels without, for all that, accomplishing any Heideggerian instituting and founding. This power of the word, at once slight and awesome, is preserved by a poetizing that insists on being "here," whose highest lucidity is the irrecusable "gray" of the day, and which does not take part in any exalted and prophetic interlocution but rather in a conversation of traces, of remembrance and witness—the traces, nevertheless, of what is life-sustaining.

> (—taggrau,
> der
> Grundwasserspuren—
>
> Verbracht
> ins Gelände
> mit
> der untrüglichen
> Spur:
> Gras,
> Gras,
> auseinandergeschrieben.)[48]

This last section, entirely in parentheses, is itself a reprise of the opening—a repetition that cannot close the circle but instead subjects the opening verses to greater fragmentation and attrition. It serves to call into question the achievement of the whole straitened duction (*Eng-führung*) traced in and as the poem. This calling into question does not come about through any *correctio* as to form, content, or vision, but through the halting reiteration of what Szondi calls the "situational determinates"—the retracing of the trace which resists all appropriation.

The duction, to summarize, led first from a time/space of refusal and from the need, as Udoff characterizes it, to cast a counter-light on the linguistic basis of memory and myth, from which the self of atrocity was formed,[49] to the fissioning disarticulation of language and to the brink of nihilism. From this failure of any coherence, however, the duction turned toward pure formal creation, the re-creation of the cosmos out of language that avoids any rhetoric of tradition, prophecy, nature, or renewal as modalities of a "poisoned silencing." Celan, however, who could not, in the end, survive his own survival, will not validate this structure of crystalline purity, within which, in Mallarmé's words, "reciprocal reflections light up like a virtual trail of sparkles across gemstones."[50] The complex precision and lucidity of such a poetics are not abandoned (nor, as Szondi puts it, "replaced and dissolved"). Celan continues, as he notes in conversation in 1966, to seek to present "excerpts of a spectrum-analysis of things," showing them in the multiplicity of their aspects, showing also how one facet veers to release another, in quasi-dialectical permutation.[51] However, this formal play, this poetic mathematics must be restored to the obscure terrain of the trace; geometry of itself (even in its Platonic version) is not ethical. It must respond to the height and the daring of the word of those who, in their extremity, transmuted the very language of brutalization into one of prayer and invocation. In the hearing of their word ("they"—as Celan himself indicated in his late poetry—are not limited to the victims of the Holocaust), Heidegger's position, that the destitution of the age remains withheld and has not, as such, come to experience and language, is untenable. In utmost abandonment and through the matrix/fencework of language (*Sprachgitter, Kristallgitter*), there arises the mandate of extending oneself toward the Other, "studying" the Other in his/her otherness—a study which Celan characterized as "my spiritual poetizing, if you will."[52] In conclusion, then, the questioning must return to the break between this "spiritual" poetics and that of Heidegger.

III

For Heidegger, a major poet's poetic saying remains obedient to its own "highest and utmost" inner necessity—an *essential* necessity to which thinking responds. The reason why this necessity, as well as the place of the interlocution between poet and thinker, must be sought for in the "unsaid" can be gleaned from Robert Bernasconi's comments concerning the "experience with language" that Heidegger seeks to make possible in his meditations on George's poem "Das Wort":

> The experience of the nothing [which "points to Being"] arises in the anxiety in which we are deprived of speech. *Nothing* is not a word for Being . . . The nothing corresponds to the thinker's experience of the lack of a word for Being. This speechlessness, this breaking of the sequence of words for Being, comes to be understood historically as marking the end of the succession of words for Being within metaphysics.[53]

An *essential* culmination and transformation is thus announced in what has failed ever to come to language but has betrayed itself through the rupture, the *caesura*. One of the circumlocutions through which Heidegger approaches this *essential* unsaid is "the word for the word." The word ("saying") lacks Being; it is not a being to which a word can be affixed, and hence it is not its *essence* as Being which has been withheld. The word is a marker of Difference, of the donation of Being out of emptiness; it brings to pass the *es gibt*, which, as Heidegger is careful to note, is divested of "the whole spook about the 'it' (*es*)."[54]

Since, on Heidegger's understanding, language or "saying" alone can accomplish the donation of Being, of the Open, and can also, in its very breakage and failure, let this donation appear as such, poetizing and thinking, as privileged forms of "saying," stand in proximity. However, this is not a proximity of assimilation, but a polemic proximity; for appropriative manifestation (*Ereignis*), which holds them in proximity, does so only by referring them to the extreme situations of "their proper over-against-each-other."

The challenge presented to the thinker by rupture or by the *caesura* is, then, as Heidegger understands it, the task of differential or polemic unification—be it of art and the technical, of Earth and World, of poetizing and thinking, or of the unconsummated past with the withheld promise of the future. This avoidance of ellipsis by differential integration is, for him, the properly spiritual task (being careful, once again, to divest the "spiritual" of spook and sentimentality).

Celan's own prominent thematization of rupture, of the possible tasks which remain for poetizing and thinking, and even of the spiritual, is at odds with Heidegger's; it does not offer the thinker points of engagement on his own terms. For Celan, the rupture that defines the contemporary situation is not *essential* but historical in its provenance. It subjects the intellectual and cultural constructs of the Western tradition, in which, of course, poetizing and thinking remain implicated, to what might be called a hermeneutics of suspicion. It refuses, furthermore, to leave language inviolate, for the word which bestows Being can veer almost imperceptibly to bestow devastation. Poet and thinker are dislodged from their normative preeminence; for this preeminence has not been ethical. What can be expected of the poet is not a wandering step and a word which defines a trail of transition from out of the darkness, but rather the "finger-thoughts" that explore the terrain of the trace to bear witness, to persevere in remembrance, and to respond to the creative word of those who dared to name what Heidegger might call the god(s) or the holy in the very situation of being, reduced to "disponible resource in the manufacture of corpses."[55]

Through the screen, the fence, and the crystalline matrix of language, Celan's poetry seeks to extend itself to the otherness of the Other, while repudiating "all oracles" and any *ess*ential unification. It seeks and needs to extend itself also to the thinker who traces the configurations of another screen. Whereas Heidegger, whose merit it is to instigate interlocution between poetizing and thinking, refused this poet the "thinking word," Levinas, the thinker of an ethics of alterity, has largely maintained intact the separation between poetry and thinking.

$$\blacklozenge$$

Meridians of Encounter

An beiden Polen
der Kluftrose, lesbar:
dein geächtetes Wort.
Nordwahr. Südhell.

        Paul Celan, "Harnischstriemen . . ." PC II, 28

At both poles
of the compass-rose of the cleft, legible:
your proscribed word.
North-true. South-bright.

In late October of 1960, Celan delivered a lecture, "Der Meridian" ("The Meridian"), in Darmstadt, on the occasion of being awarded the Georg Büchner prize for literature.[1] Otto Pöggeler attests that Celan had written reams of drafts before finally composing the lecture, in its cryptic brevity, within the space of a few days. The text bears every mark of having been *verdichtet*—condensed, intensified, strained, and carried to the very limits of prose communication. In Pöggeler's words, Celan could only "lay out a few fish-hooks" with which to catch hold of what had been the sustained concern of intellectual conversations as well as solitary reflection.[2] In Heidegger's parlance, this concern can be described as one for the *essential* origin of the work of art and for the identity and role of the poet in a destitute time.

Celan's text shows the evident, if eroded, traces of intensive dialogue not only with the living but also with the dead—with Büchner, Lenz, Benjamin, Mallarmé, Kafka, Mandelstamm, Schestow, and even Pascal and Malebranche—but the name written, so to speak, in invisible ink throughout and across the text is that of Heidegger. Celan problematizes important Heideggerian thought-structures concerning the relationship of poetry to art and language and of art to technicity and historicity, concerning language and the Open, the tracing out of paths, and finally, concerning interlocution itself.

Pöggeler recalls the fact that a lecture series, "Language," organized by the Bavarian Academy of Fine Arts, took place the year before (1959). Heidegger and Martin Buber (another unsigned partner in the dialogue instigated by Celan) were participants, the former contributing "The Way to Language," which followed closely (both in time and thematically) upon "The *Essence* of Language" and "The Word" (GA 12, 229–257; 149–204; 207–225). In April of 1961, Pöggeler presented a copy of "Der Meridian" to Heidegger, with whom he subsequently engaged in discussions of the text, which formed part of a sustained interchange (lasting from 1959 to 1972) on Celan's poetry and poetics.[3] Nonetheless (as already noted in chapter 6), none of Heidegger's published writings address Celan's art or thought.

Apart from Pöggeler's indications and Lacoue-Labarthe's pioneering work in *La poésie comme expérience*,[4] Celan's intense engagement with Heidegger in "Der Meridian" has gone unnoticed. A careful analysis of this cryptic text as not only a singular poetic document but also as a somewhat encrypted interlocution, or indeed, confrontation with Heidegger still remains to be undertaken. To carry out such a study today—at a time approaching the thirtieth anniversary of the original occasion—calls for more than an exegesis: it requires a widening of the scope of interlocution to include new interlocutors who speak out of a concern for Heidegger's politics, notably Lacoue-Labarthe and Derrida.[5] As a fitting conclusion to the present book, with its focus on *poiēsis, sophia, technē*, such a study is undertaken here.

I

What is at issue for Celan in "Der Meridian" is the self-presentation of art, its inter-involvement with *technē* and politics, and finally, the relationship between poetry (*Dichtung*) and art. High-culture conversations about art, he notes at the outset, could be continued indefinitely (if perhaps with a sterility foreshadowed by the story of Pygmalion) if "something did not intervene."

The (political) intervention, however, "penetrates inconsiderately"; it certainly puts an end to the Romantic construals of art as "glowing," "driven," or "radiant" creation. Nevertheless, it does not (*pace* Plato) banish art; it restores it, rather, in "a more ashen storm-light," namely in the "ape's form" of *mimēsis*. One needs to recall here Lacoue-Labarthe's painstaking analysis of the aesthetization of the political, which defines the very program of National Socialism, and, in particular, of the mimetic *agon* that, within this aesthetization, bound the future of Germany to ancient Greece.[6]

Finally, Celan indicates, art returns in a third and closely linked guise, the guise of the automaton, of *technē*. It is announced as such by the mechanical and "rasping" voice of Büchner's Valerio, as "nothing but artifice and mechanism, nothing but glued-on covers and watch-springs."[7] It is *technē* itself which has become apophantic, which as "the sur-plus of *physis*" allows the latter to decipher and represent itself (HAP, 69). In virtue of these substitutions, there remains, as Celan observes ironically, much to say about art; the cultured conversation has not exhausted itself.

Someone may, nevertheless, listen to and participate in this sustained conversation without seeming to understand—someone who is "artblind" because s/he insists on hearing the poetic word as "breath, which means direction, and destiny" (PC III, 1888). Destiny is not thought here—as for Heidegger—through the recreation of history on the stage of myth; nor does it assign to the poetic word a foundational (or any other) role in constituting the political as a total work of art (*Gesamtkunstwerk*)—a conception that Lacoue-Labarthe has perceptively identified as the political model of National Socialism (HAP, 64). The destinal orientation tends, rather, toward a space of freedom that is the gap of the *caesura*—a space where no tradition consummates itself but which is opened up by a word that renders homage to "the majesty of the absurd which attests to the presence of the human" (PC III, 190). With reference to Büchner's play, *Danton's Death*, Celan points to the figure of Lucile, who, standing by the guillotine through which her revolutionary husband, Camille Desmoulins, died his death "theatrically," even "iambically," shouts suddenly and incongruously: "Long live the king!" Such a "counter-word," Celan observes, "has no name which is permanently fixed; but I believe it is—poetry" (PC III, 190). Celan, first of all, disagrees here sharply with Heidegger's conception of language as speaking out of itself and saying the enigma of manifestation; Lucile speaks the counter-word because, as one who is "artblind," she perceives language under the aspect of the human.

Furthermore, Celan marks a rupture between poetry and art, whereas Heidegger, who considers language to be "poetry in the *essential* sense," also insists that art is in *essence* poetry (*Dichtung*), understood as the instituting or the "lighting projection" of truth (GA 5, 60–63). This relationship, in Heidegger's view, gives poetry in the usual sense (*Poesie*) a certain privilege among the arts. Can the interval which opens up for Celan, the interval between the "puppet-stage" and the counter-word, be bridged by a naturalizing of art? Büchner, after all, had already rejected academic formalism and "idealism" and considered a feeling for life to be the most important criterion of art; and it is here, Celan notes, that one must seek the social and political roots of Büchner's writing (PC III, 191). Would such a naturalization then place art in its entirety under the aspect of the human? Would it set at ease a poet who is constrained to consider art "under the acute accent of the contemporary" and who admits that he cannot disengage himself from something "which seems to be connected with art" (namely, what has here been referred to as the aesthetization of the political)?

There is, however, no art without *poiésis*—which is, of course, what enables Heidegger to insist on the original bond between art and *technē* and to assert that a meaningful engagement with technicity will have to take place in a domain at once related to the technical and fundamentally different from it.[8] Art cannot be straightforwardly naturalized, because it marks the technical detour or supplement through which *physis* contemplates and completes itself. As Celan remarks with reference to Büchner's *Lenz*: "'One would wish to be a Medusa's head' . . . so as to grasp the natural as natural by means of art" (PC III, 192). This shared insistence on the fundamentally technical character of art and on its supplementary relationship to nature is here the key point of Celan's engagement with Heidegger's thought.

Whereas the essential connection between art and *technē*/technicity supports, for Heidegger, the thought of a possible salutary historical transition, of "saving" growing in the midst of "danger," for Celan it opens upon the panorama of the most ancient, yet also the most contemporary, "uncanniness." Art, he notes, requires a departure from the human, an entry into a realm which is both "turned towards man and uncanny—the same in which the ape's form, the automata, and therewith . . . alas, art as well appear to be at home" (PC III, 192). Celan had already obliquely indicated the uncanniness of this connection in his poem "Todesfuge" (published in the 1948 collection *Der Sand aus den Urnen*, and subsequently retracted from publication) by showing death presented in the death camps as an artistic-technical "master from Germany." It is under the "acute accent" of the contemporary that one is driven to reopen the question of the relation between art, poetry, and *technē*, that one must ask, specifically:

> Can we—as is done in many places—start out from art as something pregiven and unconditionally to be presupposed; should we, to put it quite concretely, above all—we say—think Mallarmé conclusively to the end? (PC III, 193)

What is called for today is rather a radical calling into question of art "from out of this orientation." A meaningful continuation of the long interrogation of art is possible in no other manner.

Since poetry must follow "the way of art" (Celan avails himself throughout of this Heideggerian trope), it cannot escape a radical calling into question. The way of art is a way of distancing, of estrangement, of putting subjectivity into abeyance—a way which therefore can readily lead on to "the Medusa's head and the automata." Poetry, like art, has to betake itself to what is strange and uncanny "with a self-forgetful I." Having thus followed the way of art, can it possibly exceed art (which is to say, the alliance between art and *technē*) and set itself free again? If so, where is one to mark the interval between art and poetry? What is the step by which poetry can exceed art and leave it behind as "the way which it has to cover, nothing less, nothing more" (PC III, 194)? What is the situation, the "place" of poetry (*Ort der Dichtung*)?

Whereas Heidegger approaches this last question as a question concerning *essential* place, which can only be defined through attentiveness to the speaking of language in the interlocution of poet and thinker, Celan, characteristically, interrogates a person in his or her life-orientation. This directionality is also sought for in the chiasm of an interconnection—that between the figure of Lenz in Büchner's narrative fragment by that title—the Lenz who "on the twentieth of January went through the mountains," and the historical Lenz who, "in the night between 23 and 24 May, 1792," was found lifeless on a Moscow street. There is here an interconnection between two sorts of interconnection: the first one, between the historical and the poetized figure or person, attests to the distancing of art, whereas the second (to be problematized in the sequel) concerns the structure of the date (in its artless factuality) as both singular and repeatable, hence capable of self-estrangement.

Where, in these multiple intersections, is the place at which Lenz, the man, the poet, was able to set himself free in his self-estrangement, to take a step which dissevered his path from the path of art? In his journey through the mountains, Büchner writes, he found it at times "inconvenient" that he could not walk on his head. Celan comments:

> He who walks on his head, ladies and gentlemen, who walks on his head, has heaven beneath him as an abyss. (PC III, 195)

It is here, in the estrangement of art, rather than in the mere factual chronicle of his life, that Lenz, the man, reveals himself; for poetry "hurries ahead"; it indicates orientation. It is also here, however, that as a poet he was able to exceed art, to set himself free. His step is a step beyond that of Lucile; for it no longer issues into sheer inversion (the counter-word) but into ellipsis—a "terrible falling silent" that cuts breath and speech. There ensues here also a *mise en abîme* of the Heideggerian mythology of the Fourfold, which disguises its inherent verticality (Earth/mortals//Heaven/divinities) beneath the complex reflections of its "mirror-play."

If poetry can issue from such a "turning of the breath" (*Atemwende*), it must follow the path of art solely for the sake of this decisive step:

> Perhaps it succeeds—since the strange and the strange, namely the abyss *and* the Medusa's head, the abyss *and* the automata, seem to lie in the same direction—perhaps it succeeds here in distinguishing between

strange and strange; perhaps here the Medusa's head shrivels; perhaps here the automata fail—for this singular short instant. (PC III, 196)

Perhaps, through the step of another estrangement, the poem can at last become free of art without being artless. To do so, however, it has to speak, to speak out of its own falling silent; and it must become capable of attesting to the alterity of that other estrangement.

II

Every poem, Celan surmises, retains within it the inscription (marked idiomatically, in the vernacular) of its "20. Jänner"; and what is new and distinctive about poems written today may be only their explicit effort to remain mindful of such dates—dates toward which and from out of which "we write ourselves" (PC III, 196). Precisely insofar as the poem is inscription, writing, or text (rather than language speaking, in the Heideggerian sense), it remains indissociable from the date.

What is it that links the poem, as a practice of writing, to the inscription of dates? To address this question, it will be necessary to examine the complex, chiasmatic structure of the date.

The date is both singular and multiple (and hence is properly neither), given that an event, in its unrepeatable singularity, can be dated only by being inscribed into multiplicity, into a series without closure. The 20th of January, for instance, returns in difference: it is the date on which Lenz began the errant wandering of his madness; it returns, therefore, both as the "date" of Hölderlin in Celan's poem "Tübingen, Jänner" (PC I, 226), and as Celan's own "date" in "Eingejännert . . ." (PC II, 351)—and it is also the date of the Wannsee Conference of 1942, the madness (*Wahn/wann*, one of Celan's wordplays) which decided the "final solution."[9] The singularity indicated by the date can be commemorated only by being effaced as such. The date, in rendering the unreadable singularity readable, also withdraws it anew from readability, rendering it, in Derrida's words, "a collocation . . . a secret configuration of memory-places."[10] Unlike Heideggerian commemoration, the commemoration facilitated by the date does not transpose the past into the future but rather interlinks past and future: the indeterminacy of the future is inscribed into the past, while the latter, nevertheless, continues to pre-scribe the future. Hence Derrida remarks that the date is a "future perfect," which is to say, "a sort of *hypothesis*, the support for a by definition unlimited number of memory-projections."[11] As the mark of a significant historical conjunction, as historical signature, the date marks the implacable resistance of the historical to hermeneutical appropriation. The date is an indicator of a sort of difference that is not ontological, for it erases Being in the position of origin:

Effacement or dissimulation, this annulment of the ring (*anneau*) of return pertains to the movement of dating. That which is to be commemorated, to be at once gathered into one and repeated, is from then on [also] at once the annihilation of the date, a sort of nothingness, or ash.[12]

The date is the mark of an inscription, which, as *in*cision, effracts pathways (in the manner of *Bahnung*),[13] but which mandates, at the same time, the *in*decision of reading (hence Derrida's thematic of *circum*cision in *Shibboleth*).[14] It therefore conjoins self-estrangement (which renders the origin unfindable) with a rigorous disruption of all totalizing moves. It shows, therein, the characteristic feature of art (which, according to Celan, creates self-estrangement; PC III, 193), while nevertheless withdrawing itself from the configuration of *technē*. If the poem, then, remains stubbornly mindful of its dates, it will, by that very token, outstrip art. For this reason Derrida can write that the enigma of the date is situated "at the crossroads between art and poetry."[15]

The poem, however, is not pure writing; it is more than text: "it speaks." It has the power of an artistically and affectively compelling communication, perhaps even of incantation. It speaks, to be sure, out of its own and "ownmost" situation and concerns, but it speaks *as a poem*, which, in remaining mindful of its dates, maintains thereby the *Andenken* of alterity. Precisely in speaking out of its ownmost, Celan notes, it may "speak *in the interest of another*, who knows, perhaps of a *wholly Other* (PC III, 196).

Celan cannot claim, with Levinas, that he is "not afraid of the word God,"[16] nor is he unwary of its Heideggerian approximations and permutations. Lest the reader/listener fail to recognize the theological problematic, however (a failure generally characteristic of interpreters of "Der Meridian"), Celan adds that this "perhaps" concerning the wholly Other is "the only thing I can, of myself and today, contribute to the old hopes," but that the poem, nevertheless, abides in hope, "a word to be referred to creation" (PC III, 196f). What is hoped for is no eschatological event or advent but rather no more and no less than the continued and renewed thinkability of a coming together of this wholly Other with a proximate Other, who is, for Celan, not only the other person but (in a significant departure from much of the Judeo-Christian tradition) also the non-human Other: "Every thing, every human being, is for the poem which orients itself towards the Other a form of the Other" (PC III, 198).

In distinction from both Heidegger and Gadamer,[17] Celan admits that the poem today comes precariously close to falling silent, that it maintains itself at the extreme margins of its own possibility, that the "vanishing" (*das Geschwinde*) which afflicts it is gaining in rapidity (*Geschwindigkeit*). Hence, one cannot say how long the "pausing of breath" (*Atempause*), which still promises the poem, can be sustained. If the poem continues to abide in expectancy, if it is still intent on the way to the Other (*unentwegt*), it does so in virtue of a speaking which is not language alone (*Sprache schlechthin*), nor yet the response (*Entsprechung*), which, for Heidegger, constitutes mortal speaking, but rather the singular voice of a human being speaking from out of the "angle of inclination" of his or her individual *Dasein* and "creatureliness." As such, it is "actualized language" that has achieved poetic form.

Such speaking addresses itself to the proximate Other, through an "attentiveness" that is not the technical accomplishment of exact observation and improved measurement for the sake of a new feat, but which Celan describes (in the words of Malebranche) as "natural prayer," and also as "a concentration which remains mindful of all our dates" (PC III, 198). Given this mindfulness, poetic "attentiveness" to the Other is in no danger of absolutizing the "ontic," in an Heideggerian oblivion of Being.

In addressing itself to the Other, in interrogating the very phenomenality (*dieses Erscheinende*) of the Other, in its attentiveness to the (potentially ominous) "tremblings" and "foreshadowings" to be gleaned from the Other, the poem becomes interlocution (*Gespräch*). Although the poem attests to the presence (*Gegenwart, Präsenz*) of a singular speaker, brings into presence that which is addressed, and has itself an "unique, punctual presence," it infuses and distends these forms of presence with alterity; in remaining mindful of its dates, it gives voice to the Other's ownmost: "the time thereof" (PC III, 199).

It would be shortsighted to conclude that Celan, in insisting that the poem maintains itself "in the enigma of encounter," dismisses Heidegger's focal concern with the enigma and structure of manifestation as lacking in ethical and politico-poetic relevance. He points out, indeed, that the interrogation of the proximate Other, in its singularity, remains oriented toward "the Open and empty and free"(PC III, 199), and that the wholly Other, turned toward the poem's speaking, is "perhaps vacant" (197). Celan, on the one hand, refuses to attribute to the singular any inherent and ultimate reality (its "ownmost" is said to be time); but on the other hand, he shows himself convinced that Heidegger's refusal to speak to the here and now, to speak as a human being addressing himself to the Face of the Other, constitutes a refusal of the "coming/word" to be expected of a thinker. This refusal also cuts short a genuine interlocution between poet and thinker (one which would respect the alterity and the "time" of the poet). It therefore frustrates the task of such an interlocution, which is to think the ethical and its intersection with the "aesthetic" as it must ultimately be thought: from out of the enigma of manifestation.

III

"The poem?", Celan pauses to ask—how can one presume to speak of the poem, absolutized like an *eidos*, "from out of *this* direction"—a direction which seeks the singular, in its alterity, in its time? A poem which remains mindful of its dates cannot be absolutized; for the date, as Derrida points out, gives "an idiom" to be thought or commemorated, to be "crossed" with and by "a possible/impossible translation."[18] The absolute poem, then, "certainly cannot be"—not even in the guise of Heidegger's "unsaid poem"—the source and reflux of the "rhythmic flow" of a singular poet's poetic saying. Hence it becomes impossible to speak meaningfully both of "the poem" and "the poet."

How is one then to think of the artifices of language that are characteristic of poetry, while being tacit or suspect, for instance, in philosophical discourse—artifices such as images, metaphors, and, more generally, tropes? All of these seem to be comparative and thus assimilative in character. In his drafts for a radio broadcast of 19 March 1960—a broadcast that attests to Celan's sustained poetic dialogue with Ossip Mandelstamm (besides Heidegger, perhaps Celan's most important interlocutor) and which importantly anticipates "Der Meridian"—Celan remarks that "the image is here no metaphor; this poetry is not an emblematic; the image has phenomenal character—it appears."[19] His point in "Der Meridian" is similar: the poem's images are "what is always again and only now and only here perceived and to be perceived" (PC III, 1999). One must, however, note the force of the "always again," which exceeds singularity, which shows the "ghostly" structure of the date, which requires, for its appearances or hauntings, the very artifice of tropes and metaphors. The poem, whatever the "shining" of its "beauty" (see chapter 1) is not blessed with sheer phenomenality: it remains art and, perhaps after all, *technē*. The metaphors and tropes, to be sure, must be carried to their breaking points to reveal the singular in the non-totalizable multiplicity of its estrangements. The poem thus shows itself as "the place where all tropes and metaphors must be carried ad absurdum" (PC III, 1999); its exploration of *topoi* (*Topos-forschung*), of man, of "creatures" can take place only "in the light of u-topia."

Celan's question of "enlarging" or surpassing art ("Elargissez l'art!"), of a possible freedom in excess of art, has in a sense led back to the beginning—to art. Every opening to excess seems to be, in the end, annexed by art, perhaps in virtue of the very conjunction of *Gestalt* with language, writing with speech. Celan's path of inquiry thus reveals itself in retrospect as "a circle," which returns, perhaps, to a Heideggerian intimacy between art and *technē*:

> Art, which is to say, the Medusa's head, mechanism, automata, that which is uncanny and so difficult to distinguish, which is, in the end, perhaps only a *single* strangeness—art lives on. (PC III, 200)

There is no other recourse, Celan finds (probably much to the dismay of an already bewildered audience), than to reopen the question concerning poetry—to pursue it again out of "another orientation."

This other orientation seeks to bypass the problematic of art, so as to look at the poem as a search for encounter and interlocution, even if only "desperate interlocution." Celan sets out on this way by recalling the narrative "Gespräch im Gebirg" ("Conversation in the Mountains"), which he wrote in 1959 (PC III, 169–173), and by citing a four-line poem "written a few years ago."[20] He notes that in both these texts he wrote himself out of a "20. Jänner"—his own "20. Jänner." The new *incipit* is, hence, once again writing, the date, the poem as text, as capable of accomplishing a decentered "annulation." However, he notes at once that poems are also ways (not the only ones) in which language "comes to voice" (*stimmhaft wird*) and extends itself genuinely to an Other, to a "you" (not necessarily different from what is all too readily called the self and presumed to be unitary) that "perceives" and that is capable of response. The poem, therefore, does not speak the language that prevails *im Gebirg* ("in the mountains"; note the Heideggerian allusion), which is "not for you and not for me," not only because the interlocutors are Jews but also because this language of the heights contains neither "I" nor "you" but only "he," "it," and "they" (even "she" is evidently excluded). It is a language not of mouth and tongue but of the stone that speaks but does not talk, addressing itself to "no-one and No-one" (PC III, 170f).

In place of such high-altitude speaking (to use here a Merleau-Pontyan term), Celan seeks a poetics of genuine interlocution, of dialogical temporalization—a sort of *bricolage*, which takes up what comes to hand, responds to it, and reconfigures it. Here, he notes, one must take special care not to fall into the error of "my countryman," Karl Emil Franzos, who, in editing Büchner's manuscripts, misread *commode* (accommodating, convenient) as *kommende* (*Religion*), that is, as what is to come. In other words, one must guard against projecting one's *bricolage* upon the horizons of the future, while nevertheless continuing to listen "beyond oneself and the words," reading their quotation marks not simply as traces ("little goose feet," a German colloquialism for quotation marks) but also as alert "little rabbit ears," which never listen quite without fear.

The exploration of *topoi* can thus be undertaken anew, proceeding at once from what is at hand and "in the light of utopia." It seeks to constitute the place of provenance as a region (*Gegend*) of encounter. Utopia, however, shows here a sinister light: the localities of provenance that define a region for Celan, Franzos, and Lenz are no longer to be found on the map—not even on the "child's map" of memory. The way that seeks them is not merely an Heideggerian "woodpath"; it is a way "into the impossible."

Something, however, is found and perhaps even "touched" at the place of this vanishing—something which, "like the poem, interconnects and leads to encounter," which is, like language, "immaterial, yet of this earth," and which, spanning both poles and crossing right through the "tropics" of tropes, returns into itself: a meridian (PC III, 202). Concerning this figure, Celan wrote to Pöggeler, in response to the latter's inquiry, that it was his concern, in "Der Meridian," to recall that dialogue (*Gespräch*), as, first of all, a reciprocity between human beings (and only then of poets), is perhaps the only "possibility" still left today.[21] A dialogue between thinker and poet is not mentioned here.

Furthermore, Celan notes, it is a question of that which is to be "rendered place" ("das 'zu Ortende'"), as "a 'place' which is 'nowhere,' yet, in each case, actual."[22] The thematic of displaced encounter yields here a spatialization of the structure of the date, which mitigates the elliptical "unavailability" of the temporal. Celan notes, finally, in the letter, that he discovered a text by Kepler which speaks of God as the sphere constituted by the totality of meridians, but of man as the circle, the single meridian. He immediately, if cryptically, problematizes this metaphysical figure of totality:

> Perhaps poems are planes of projection of this "hyper-ouranian place," significant-"uninterpretable" in virtue of the pneumatic outline sketch which falls to their lot . . . when they keep themselves open to what is above and below.[23]

Finally, after a shift to the figure of connected or "communicating" pipes (in which water stands at the same level), Celan concludes: "Or quite simply, there is love and its receptacles."[24]

The figure of the meridian reappears in sharper focus, with reference to Mandelstamm, in Celan's poem "Und mit dem Buch aus Tarussa," from the 1963 collection *Die Niemandsrose*:

> Gross
> geht der Verbannte dort oben, der
> Verbrannte, ein Pommer, zuhause
> im Maikäferlied, das mütterlich blieb, sommerlich, hell-
> blütig am Rand
> aller schroffen,
> winterhart-kalten
> Silben.
> Mit ihm
> wandern die Meridiane:
> an-
> gesogen von seinem
> sonnengesteuerten Schmerz, der die Länder verbrüdert nach

dem Mittagsspruch einer
liebenden
Ferne . . .[25]

Although the poem is singular and speaks to the singular, its meridian-course is a cosmic one, "sun-steered," interlinking what is dissevered, like the Platonic *erōs* (to which Celan's "flügge / von Wunden" ["fledged / by wounds"] may also allude). From out of the midnight darkness of exile and devastation, it pronounces its "noonday saying" of a love that reaches through distances.

The meridian is a figure which has no Heideggerian analogue. The pole, for Heidegger, is the singular pole or pivot of manifestation, around which the *polis* configures itself as an "essential site" of historical human dwelling.[26] The *polis* is thought in aletheic terms, rather than in terms of human polarizations and their possible reconciliation. Celan's vision, by contrast, remains more closely attuned to Plato's, for whom it is ultimately *erōs* that makes possible the accomplishment of *arētē* in the *polis* (*Symp.*, 212a). Celan, however, replaces Plato's structure of intellectual ascent by what one might call the complex crystallography of his poetics.

In Celan's late and last poetry, nevertheless, the poles reassert their power of disseverance. They are spoken of, in one of the series of poems which sprang from Celan's 1969 journey to Israel, as "in us, / insurmountable / in waking."[27] Neither a mysticism of love nor yet the subtle rigor of Celan's poetics could, in the end, sustain their projection of meridians of human encounter against the weight of experience, in isolation from a philosophical questioning of the nature of manifestation. Although, in Heidegger's texts that engage with the poets, this questioning is often amalgamated with his reactionary yet prophetic crypto-politics, it remains—to the extent that it can be freed of this torsion—his invaluable contribution to the interlocution and, indeed, to a wide range of contemporary discourse.

Postscript

◆

The studies that make up this book trace, throughout Heidegger's readings of his chosen poets, a persistent deflection toward *essentialization* and toward a unification which masks itself as being "polemic" and thus differential. This unifying tendency operates in several registers: (1) with regard to the supposed unicity and homogeneity of any given poetic text; (2) as concerns the single and withdrawn source of the poet's articulation; (3) with respect to an *essential* mandate shared by the major poets of Germany and ancient Greece; and finally, (4) as concerns the conjunction of poetry and thinking in their response to the crisis of epochal closure. Heidegger cannot countenance poetry as a tenuous writing against loss (as it shows itself in Hölderlin and certainly in Trakl), nor as refractory to destinal constructs. Moreover, he cannot speak to the contemporary situation of poetry, to what both Adorno and Celan problematize as its very possibility and possible identity in the wake of the Shoah. Poetry today is no more in continuity with its tradition than thinking is in continuity with metaphysics.

Specifically, Heidegger fails to address the fact that the disclosive power of the poetic word has been profoundly affected, if not despoiled, by history, as have the mythic symbols and intellectual constructs of the Western tradition and, indeed, language itself, which, in Celan's poetry, is brought to betray both its opacity and its sinister powers. These structures call, therefore, for a vigilant hermeneutics of suspicion rather than an *essential* consummation of the 19th-century project of retrieval that still informs Heidegger's readings.

Celan delineates two itineraries that remain open to poetry in its contemporary situation. The first acknowledges that poetry is artifice or *technē* and seeks to "think Mallarmé to the end," by developing a purely formalist poetics and constructing for poetry a crystalline cosmos of aesthetic self-sufficiency. Whereas Heidegger would repudiate such an understanding of poetry as devoid of *essential* vision (and Gadamer would insist on the impossibility of a purely formalist poetics), Celan eventually rejects it for its failure of commemoration and of establishing an ethical relationship to the Other.

The second avenue of orientation seeks to restore poetry to the "day-gray" of history and of human encounter, to render it utterly attentive and responsive to the Other in its singularity. By eroding poetry's aesthetic self-containment through the time of the Other, Celan strives to dissever it from *poiēsis* and *technē*. He recognizes, however, that such disseverance requires that poetry outstrip (rather than bypass) art, by carrying the very tropes of its artifice to the breaking point, the point of their subversion. He seeks to push it to this breaking point by keeping the poem faithful to its singular "dates" (see chapter 7) and allowing the very structure of the date to disrupt all totalizing moves. What Celan's effort to resituate poetry turns and eventually founders on is Heidegger's own crucial problematic of *technē*.

Precisely because of its *essential* character of *poiēsis*, and thus its kinship to technicity, Heidegger sees in art the still unconsummated possibility of motivating an epochal turning (*Kehre*) away from the reductive totalization characteristic of technicity, and toward a modality of disclosure responsive to the event-character of manifestation. Poetry is therefore, for him, the precursor or trail-blazer of a thinking that conforms itself to the event-like temporality of presencing (*anwesen*), rather than seeking to define and legitimate the modalities of the presence (*Anwesenheit*) of what presences. Heidegger insists on both the actional or *praxis*-character of such a thinking and its necessity and saving power in the face of the distress and "utmost danger" that attend the contemporary interpretive configuration (planetary technicity). However, Heidegger's privileging of art and *poiēsis*, as the hidden truth of the political (given that, from the 1930s on, he regards *praxis* as political in nature), is also of crucial importance as concerns his involvement with National Socialism. Lacoue-Labarthe argues this point perceptively:

> But if this essence of the political is to be sought in art, no aesthetic, nor any philosophy of art either, is capable of undoing the unseverable link between art and politics, because its categories . . . have at their roots the presupposition . . . that the political ("religion") is the truth of art. This is why Heidegger, in so far as his project in the 1930s explicitly consists in "overcoming" aesthetics, gives a privileged access . . . to the essence of the political that is simultaneously veiled and unveiled by National Socialism. (HAP, 77)

Celan problematizes, in the technical detour that he finds indissociable from art, not only a certain distancing from the compelling immediacy of experience and from ethical responsibility but, more importantly, an alliance with "the most ancient uncanniness." The latter may be interpreted as the self-production (*auto-poiēsis*) not only of the subject (as characteristic of modernity), but also of collective identities—a self-production in league with practices of exclusion and domination. The technical detour which renders art possible is also, as both Hölderlin and Celan saw clearly, the supplementation by which *physis* completes itself, so as to accomplish *apophansis*. Lacoue-Labarthe must be credited, once again, for clarifying this structure of "originary secondarity," and for pointing out the close alliance between what Heidegger calls *Sage*, which is the wellspring of *poiēsis*, and the mythization which enables self-production (see HAP, 84).

Celan hence strives to interrupt art, to bring poetry to set itself free by exceeding art, by repudiating all mythization and "oracles," while situating itself in the "day-gray" of actuality, and, above all, by letting itself be claimed by "another estrangement," which is that of alterity. Whereas Heidegger seeks to counter rampant nihilism with *essential* thinking or aletheic mindfulness, Celan finds the Archimedean point of his resistance to nihilism in what is at once momentous and minimal: in the humanity and spirituality maintained by those who died in degradation, in the hymning by the "buried wall" (see "Engführung"), as contrasted with the hymning of "the German" (*das Deutsche*). Celan, however, despairs in the end of thus setting poetry free, of achieving a poetic commemoration and communication that would decisively resist annexation by *technē*.

If such annexation continues to reassert itself, one has cause to question Heidegger's guiding conviction that technicity contains within itself the hidden yet *essential* momentum for its own subversion, a subversion which consists in the releasement of un-principled presencing, and that, moreover, this subversion can be brought about through a conjunction of *essential* thinking with poetry at the decisive time of epochal closure.

There is, however, a crucial aspect of this Heideggerian thought-structure which is all too easily and frequently overlooked: his conviction that *physis* does not complete itself, through its poetic supplement, by un-concealing presences or their modalities of presence, but ultimately by un-concealing its very withdrawal, its refusal to legitimate any posit, its "emptiness," as thematized in this book. The inconspicuousness (quite literally, the non-specularity) of this withdrawal is precisely what renders a thinking in quest of it so prone to annexation by mythical constructs.

Given Celan's own relationship to Hölderlin's poetics, the failure of his attempted interlocution with Heidegger implicates Heidegger's interlocution with the poets in its entirety. An important, twofold reason for this failure is Heidegger's neglect and obscuring of the ethical import of the responsive relationship between human being and the enigma of manifestation, together with Celan's refusal to countenance a quasi-ontological meditation as being ethically responsible and, indeed, indispensable for the articulation of an ethics of alterity.

The ethical, as here understood, is not in continuity with the "principled" ethical analyses and systems of the philosophical tradition, which have reached the point of their exhaustion in the "death-event" (Wyschogrod's term) of the 20th century. It substitutes releasement or "letting be" for normative injunctions, principles, and rules. Notwithstanding its initial appearance of weakness, the injunction to "let be" is, in fact, as Silvia Benso (one of the very few scholars, so far, to consider these issues) writes, possessed of "an innovating charge whose characters are explosive and devastating with regard to the instituted order."[1] Schürmann (whose focus is on *praxis* rather than on ethics) has clearly shown that to let technicity be is the very *praxis* which can push it to its subversion, and that such *praxis* forms a practical a priori without which *essential* thinking "lapses into impossibility."[2] This book moves toward the conclusion that what Heidegger's interlocution with the poets calls for is an articulation of the chiasm linking the ontological and ethical aspects of alterity, namely, responsiveness to the enigma of manifestation and responsibility for the Other.

Notes

◆

INTRODUCTION

1. Maurice Merleau-Ponty, *The Visible and the Invisible*, Alphonso Lingis, trans. (Evanston: Northwestern University Press, 1968), 197.
2. M. Heidegger, "Die Herkunft der Kunst und die Bestimmung des Denkens," lecture presented on 4 April 1967 at the Academy for Science and Arts in Athens. I translate and cite from a copy of Heidegger's typescript. The text is available in French translation by Jean-Louis Chrétien and Michèle Reifenbach, "La provenance de l'art et la détermination de la pensée," in Michel Haar, ed., *L'Herne: Heidegger* (Paris: Editions de l'Herne, 1983), 84–92.
3. "Die Herkunft der Kunst" (unpaginated). For Heidegger's earlier development of this thought, see his 1935 essay "Der Ursprung des Kunstwerkes," *Holzwege*, GA 5, 1–74. English translation by Albert Hofstadter, "The Origin of the Work of Art," in *Martin Heidegger: Poetry, Language, Thought*, A. Hofstadter, ed. (New York: Harper & Row, 1971), 15–87. To be referred to as PLT.
4. "Der Ursprung des Kunstwerkes," 59f; PLT 71ff.
5. M. Heidegger, *Einführung in die Metaphysik*, 3rd ed. (Tübingen: Niemeyer, 1976), 29. English translation by Ralph Mannheim, *An Introduction to Metaphysics* (Garden City, N.Y.: Doubleday, 1961).
6. Philippe Lacoue-Labarthe, *Heidegger, Art and Politics*, Chris Turner, trans. (Oxford: Blackwell, 1990).
7. Emmanuel Levinas, *Totality and Infinity*, Alphonso Lingis, trans. (Pittsburgh: Duquesne University Press, 1969), 45.
8. Reiner Schürmann, "Riveted to a Monstrous Site: On Heidegger's *Beiträge zur Philosophie*," paper presented at a conference on Heidegger and Practical Life, Greater Philadelphia Philosophy Consortium, 18 March 1989.

CHAPTER 1. PHAINESTHAI, BEAUTY, SEMBLANCE: READING MÖRIKE

1. See Berel Lang and Christine Ebel, trans., "A 1951 Dialogue on Interpretation: Emil Staiger, Martin Heidegger, Leo Spitzer," *PMLA* 105:3 (May, 1990), 409–485. This translation includes "The Art of Interpretation," the Heidegger/Staiger correspondence, and Leo Spitzer's article, "Once again on Mörike's Poem 'Auf eine Lampe,'" together with Spitzer's "Addendum" and Staiger's

115

"Response." It will be referred to as "Dialogue." The exchange provoked by Staiger's lecture was originally published in *Trivium*, 9 (1951), 1–16; 133–157.

Staiger's summary of his lecture (which is not included in the translation) and the exchange of letters between Heidegger and Staiger are published in M. Heidegger, *Aus der Erfahrung des Denkens (1910–1976)*, GA 13, 93–109.

2. Staiger explains that he understands rhythm in the sense of Gustav Becking's *Der musikalische Rhythmus als Erkenntnisquelle*, namely, as the inner law and source of artistic configuration. See p. 417 of the *Dialogue*. In "Die Sprache im Gedicht," *Unterwegs zur Sprache*, GA 12, 34, Heidegger describes rhythm as the aesthetic representation of "the place of the poem . . . as the source of the way-making wave [of a given poet's poetic 'saying']."

3. On 27 July 1882, Mörike visited Hölderlin in Tübingen in the company of two friends. He read *Hyperion* in 1925 with Mährlen. Vischer, Mörike's "intellectual broker," visited the infirm Hölderlin several times. For details of these contacts, see the "Chronology" of the Frankfurt Edition of Hölderlin, *Sämtliche Werke*, vol. 9.

4. "Still undisplaced, oh beautiful lamp, you adorn, / by light chains gracefully suspended here, / the ceiling of the now almost forgotten festive room. / Upon your white marble bowl whose rim / the ivy wreath of gold-green bronze entwines, / a band of children gaily links up for the roundelay. / How charming it all is! Laughing, yet a gentle spirit / of seriousness flows 'round the entire form. / An art-work of the genuine kind. Who gives it heed? / But what is beautiful shines blessedly in itself."

(My translation of the poem follows Heidegger's reading of the last verse rather than Staiger's.)

5. Staiger, "Dialogue," 417.

6. Ibid., 420.

7. Ibid., 421f.

8. Whereas Heidegger uses the Greek term *symbolon* (token, sign, or signal), Hegel uses the German *Symbol* and characterizes it as "an external existence immediately available or given to intuition which, however, is not to be taken as it immediately is present before one, on its own terms, but rather in a broader and more general sense." See G. W. F. Hegel, *Vorlesungen über die Aesthetik*, I; "Jubiläumsausgabe," Hermann Glockner, ed., 4th ed. (Stuttgart/Bad Cannstatt: Friedrich Fromann, 1964), vol. 12, 407–421.

9. Compare here M. Heidegger, "Der Ursprung des Kunstwerkes," 'Die Wahrheit und die Kunst,' GA 5.

10. Hegel, *Vorlesungen über die Aesthetik*, 28.

11. Ibid., 164.

12. Ibid., 20.

13. Staiger, "Dialogue," 422f.

14. Ibid., 423–436.

15. Ibid., 423.

16. M. Heidegger, *Sein und Zeit*, 12th ed. (Tübingen: Niemeyer, 1972), 27–38. English translation by J. Macquarrie and E. Robinson, *Being and Time* (New York: Harper & Row, 1962).

17. See Heidegger, "Der Ursprung des Kunstwerkes" ("The Origin of the Work of Art").

18. Staiger, "Dialogue," 426.

19. Ibid., 426f.

20. For a scholarly discussion of the whole exchange, see David Halliburton, *Poetic Thinking: An Approach to Heidegger* (Chicago: University of Chicago Press, 1981), ch. 3.
21. For a discussion of the thing-poem, see Rudolf Dirk Schier, *Die Sprache Georg Trakls* (Heidelberg: C. Winter, 1970).
22. Staiger, "Dialogue," 429.
23. "Where the sun in its fiery radiance hemmed the shaded circle / measuring almost equally, 'round about with a blinding border . . .'"
24. M. Heidegger, "Logos (Heraklit, Fragment 50)," *Vorträge und Aufsätze*, III, 3–25. English translation by David Farrell Krell and Frank A. Capuzzi, "Logos (Heraclitus Fragment B 50)," in *Martin Heidegger: Early Greek Thinking* (New York: Harper & Row, 1975), 59–78.
25. Heidegger, "Logos," 8; 64.
26. Ibid., 25; 78.
27. See Reiner Schürmann, *Heidegger on Being and Acting; from Principles to Anarchy*, trans. Christine-Marie Gros (Bloomington: Indiana University Press, 1982), 170f.
28. M. Heidegger, "Aus einem Gespräch von der Sprache (1953/54): Zwischen einem Japaner und einem Fragenden," GA 12, 79–146. The identification of the partners in dialogue as "a Japanese" and "one who questions" is interesting in terms of what is nowadays called "the colonial gaze." English translation by Peter D. Hertz and Joan Stambaugh, "A Dialogue on Language," in *On the Way to Language*, P. D. Hertz and J. Stambaugh, eds. (New York: Harper & Row, 1971).
29. The Greeks, Heidegger notes in "Logos," were *situated* in the understanding of *logos* which he explicates, but they were unable to "think" it. Hence they represented language as *phone* and *glossa*, initiating the whole tradition known in deconstructive parlance as phonologocentrism.
30. "Die Sprache," GA 12, 10–30; "Language," PLT, 189–210.
31. Heidegger, "Logos," 21; 75.
32. See Yasuo Yuasa, "The Encounter of Modern Japanese Philosophy with Heidegger," in *Heidegger and Asian Philosophy*, Graham Parkes, ed. (Honolulu: University of Hawaii Press, 1987), 155–174.
33. *Anmut* is properly translated as "charm" or "grace" rather than as "enchantment"; but the latter translation does justice to Tezuka's idiosyncratic usage.
34. Heidegger, " . . . dichterisch wohnet der Mensch . . .," *Vorträge und Aufsätze*, II (Pfullingen: Neske, 1967), 61–78. English translation by Albert Hofstadter, ". . . Poetically Man Dwells . . .," PLT, 213–229.

CHAPTER 2. SITUATING HEIDEGGER SITUATING GEORG TRAKL

1. See M. Heidegger, "Die Frage nach der Technik," *Vorträge und Aufsätze*, I (Pfullingen: Neske, 1967), 5–36, and "Die Kehre," in *Die Technik und die Kehre*, *Opuscula*, I (Pfullingen: Neske, 1985), 37–47. The latter text contains both essays. English translation of the first essay by William Lovitt, "The Question Concerning Technology," in *Basic Writings* (New York: Harper & Row, 1977), 287–317. To be referred to as BW.
2. See M. Heidegger, "Wozu Dichter?," *Holzwege*, GA 5, 269–320 (271, 294, 319). English translation by Albert Hofstadter, "What are Poets for?," PLT, 91–142.

3. See M. Heidegger, *Die Selbstbehauptung der deutschen Universität*, republished, together with *Das Rektorat: Tatsachen und Gedanken* (Frankfurt a. M.: Klostermann, 1983). An English translation of these texts, by Karsten Harries, "The Self-Assertion of the German University," appears in *Review of Metaphysics*, 38 (March, 1985), 467–502. Cf. also Heidegger's letter to the Academic Rectorate of the Albert-Ludwig University, 4 November 1945, available in the French translation of J. M. Vaysse in *L'Herne: Martin Heidegger*, Michel Haar, ed. (Paris: Editions de l'Herne, 1983), 100–103.

4. Heidegger's discussion of Trakl's poetry is found in "Die Sprache" and "Die Sprache im Gedicht," *Unterwegs zur Sprache*, GA 12, 7–30, 31–78. "Die Sprache" appears in Hofstadter's translation as "Language," PLT, 187–210. For a translation of the second essay, "Language in the Poem," see Peter D. Hertz and Joan Stambaugh, trans., *On the Way to Language* (New York: Harper & Row, 1971). For a discussion of Trakl's relationship to Hölderlin, see Bernhard Böschenstein, "Hölderlin und Rimbaud, simultane Rezeption als Quelle poetischer Innovation im Werk Georg Trakls," *Salzburger Trakl-Symposion*, Walter Weiss and Hans Weichselbaum, eds. (Salzburg: Otto Müller Verlag, 1978), 9–27.

5. Kathleen Wright, "Reading Heidegger Reading Hölderlin," paper given at a conference on "Art, Politics, Technology: Martin Heidegger, 1889–1989" at Yale University, October 1989. An expanded version of the paper is to be published in the conference proceedings, ed. K. Harries and O. Pöggeler. I am grateful to Professor Wright for making her paper available to me.

6. See Georg Trakl's letters to Erhard Buschbeck and to Kurt Wolff Verlag from April 1913 to June 1914. These can be found in *Georg Trakl: Dichtungen und Briefe*, 2 vols., Walther Killy and Hans Szklenar, eds. (Salzburg: Otto Müller Verlag, 1969), I, 241–318. Trakl's poetry is cited from this edition.

7. I am indebted to a discussion of this Hölderlin figure in an unpublished manuscript by Glenn W. Most, "Hölderlin and the Poetry of History."

8. Wright, "Reading Heidegger Reading Hölderlin," 6.

9. Reiner Schürmann, *Heidegger on Being and Acting: From Principles to Anarchy*, 267.

10. Bernhard Böschenstein, "Hölderlin und Rimbaud," 15. See also Böschenstein's contributions to the working discussions in *Salzburger Trakl-Symposion*, 106f.

11. Russell E. Brown, "The Motif of Uncertainty in Trakl's Poetry," *Internationales Trakl-Symposium*, Joseph P. Strelka, ed., "Internationales Jahrbuch für Germanistik," A XII (Berne: Peter Lang, 1984), 46–66 (47).

12. Böschenstein, "Hölderlin und Rimbaud," 10–14. Compare, in particular, Trakl's poem "Helian."

13. "Over the white pond / the wild birds have flown away. / In the evening there blows from our stars an icy wind. // Over our tombs / bends the broken forehead of night. / Under oak-trees we rock in a silver boat. // Always there resound the white walls of the city. / Under thorn-arches / oh my brother we climb blind pointers toward midnight."

14. Jacques, Derrida, *De l'esprit: Heidegger et la question* (Paris: Editions Galilée, 1987), ch. viii.

15. Ibid., 19.

16. See Heidegger, "The Self-Assertion of the German University."

17. See Heidegger, *Letter to the Academic Rectorate of the Albert-Ludwig University*. I have consulted this document in the French translation of J. M. Vaysse (see note 4).

18. Heidegger, "The Self-Assertion," 470.
19. Ibid., 474–476.
20. Wright, "Reading Heidegger Reading Hölderlin," 10. For Heidegger's distinction between the poet's "grounding" (*begründen*) and the thinker's "conquering" (*erobern*) of the "Fatherland," see his *Hölderlins Hymnen "Germanien" und "Der Rhein,"* Susanne Ziegler, ed., GA 39, pp. 4f, 51, 144. Compare to this Heidegger's later distinction between the poet's "founding" (*gründen*) and the thinker's "instituting" (*stiften*) of history in his lecture course *Hölderlins Hymne "Andenken,"* Curd Ochwadt, ed., GA 52, 3.
21. Karl Löwith, *Mein Leben in Deutschland vor und nach 1933* (Stuttgart: Metzler, 1986), 57.
22. "The wanderer quietly enters; / pain has petrified the threshold. / There shine forth in pure brightness / upon the table bread and wine."
23. See M. Heidegger, "'Only a God Can Save Us': The *Spiegel* Interview," Wm. J. Richardson, S. J., trans., in Thomas Sheehan, ed., *Heidegger: The Man and the Thinker* (Chicago: Precedent Publishing, Inc., 1981), 43–71 (58, 60).
24. See Paul de Man, *Allegories of Reading* (New Haven: Yale University Press, 1978), 227, and Jacques Derrida, *De l'esprit*, 146ff, for a discussion of this notion. Heidegger's own thematization of *Versprechen*, however, has gone unheeded. Critics who read the locution *die Sprache spricht* as attesting to linguistic mysticism or absolutism fail to see that such *(ver)sprechen* functions in a manner similar to Derrida's notion of *espacement* (spacing).
25. Heidegger, "Die Frage nach der Technik," 32.
26. Böschenstein, "Hölderlin und Rimbaud," 15–19.
27. "Outcry in sleep; through dark alleys the wind plunges; / the blue of springtime hints through breaking branches; / crimson night-dew, and all around the stars are extinguished. / Greenish dawns the river, silver the old avenues / and the towers of the city. Oh gentle drunkenness / in the gliding boat, and the dark calls of the thrush / in childlike gardens. Already the rosy veil lightens. // Solemnly the waters rustle. Oh the moist shadows of the meadow, / the striding animal. Greening things, flower-branches / touch the crystal forehead; shimmering, rocking boat. / Great is the silence of the spruce forest, the earnest shadows by the river. // Purity! Purity! Where are the fearsome paths of death, / of the gray, stony silences, the rocks of the night / and the unquiet shadows? Radiant abyss of the sun. // Sister, when I found you in the solitary clearing / of the forest and it was noon and great the animal's silence, / white one under wild oak, and silver the thorn flowered. / Vehement dying and the singing flame in the heart. // More darkly the waters flow around the beautiful games of fishes. / Hour of mourning, silent regard of the sun; / something strange upon earth the soul is. Spiritually there dawns / blueness above the mutilated forest and there tolls / long a dark bell in the village, peaceable escort. / Quietly the myrtle flowers above the white eyelids of the dead one. // Softly the waters resound in the sinking afternoon / and more darkly there greens the wilderness by the bank, joy in the rosy wind. / The gentle song of the brother upon the evening hill."

CHAPTER 3. THE SPHERE AND THE BALL: RILKE'S (DIS)FIGURATION

1. M. Heidegger, *Parmenides* (*Wintersemester 1942/43*), GA 54 (1982).
2. *Das über-setzende Wort*. The hyphen brings out Heidegger's play on the ordinary meaning (the translating word) and the literal-etymological meaning (the word crossing over). For a discussion, see Manfred Frings, *"Parmenides*: Heidegger's 1942/43 Lecture Held at Freiburg University," *Journal of the British Society for Phenomenology*, 19:1 (January 1988), 15–33.
3. For a discussion, see Véronique M. Fóti, "*Alētheia* and Oblivion's Field: On Heidegger's Parmenides Lectures," in Charles E. Scott and Arleen Dallery, eds., *Ethics and Danger: Currents in Continental Thought*; "Selected Studies in Phenomenology and Existential Philosophy" (1989), forthcoming, 1991.
4. M. Heidegger, "Wozu Dichter?," GA 5.
5. Cf. Heidegger, "Der Spruch des Anaximander," GA 5, 206–243. English translation by David Farrell Krell and Frank Capuzzi, "The Anaximander Fragment," in *Early Greek Thinking*, 13–58.
6. For a discussion, see Edith Wyschogrod, *Spirit in Ashes: Hegel, Heidegger, and Man-Made Mass Death* (New Haven and London: Yale University Press, 1985), ch. 6.
7. "Wozu Dichter," 278. See also Véronique M. Fóti, "Representation and the Image: Between Derrida, Heidegger, and Plato," *Man and World*, 18 (1985), 65–78.
8. Werner Hamacher, "The Second of Inversion: Movements of a Figure through Celan's Poetry," *The Lesson of Paul de Man*, ed. Peter Brooks, et al., *Yale French Studies*, 69 (1985), 276–311.
9. From a letter by Rilke to Countess Sizzo, dated by Heidegger 6 January 1923, but in fact dated 1 June 1923. See *Materialen zu Rainer Maria Rilkes "Duineser Elegien,"* U. Füllborn and M. Engel, ed. (Frankfurt a. M.: Suhrkamp, 1980), 280–284.
10. Paul de Man, "Tropes (Rilke)," *Allegories of Reading*, 20–56.
11. Cf. M. Heidegger, "Vom Wesen der Wahrheit," *Wegmarken*, GA 9, 73–97, and "Der Ursprung des Kunstwerkes," GA 5, 7–68.
12. "All is vast—, and nowhere does the circle close. / See in the bowl, upon the gaily laid table, / [how] strange the faces of fish. // Fish are mute—one used to think. Who knows? But isn't there at last a place where what would be / the language of fish is spoken, *without* them?"

    R. M. Rilke, *Sonnets to Orpheus*, II:20. Cited from *Sämtliche Werke*, Ernst Zinn, ed. (Zürich: Insel Verlag, 1956), I, 764f. I have consulted A. Poulin, Jr.'s, translations, *Rilke: Duino Elegies and the Sonnets to Orpheus* (Boston: Houghton Mifflin Co., 1977), but have departed from his renderings, mostly in the interest of literality.
13. de Man, *Allegories of Reading*, 47.
14. See Friedrich W. Wodtke's discussion, with reference to Hoffmannsthal and Klopstock, in "Das Problem der Sprache bein späten Rilke," in Rüdiger Gorner, ed., *Rainer Maria Rilke* (Darmstadt: Wissenschaftliche Buchgesellscaft, 1987), 78–130.
15. *Rilke to Ellen Delp*, 27 November 1915, in *Materialen zu Rainer Maria Rilkes "Duineser Elegien,"* 132f.
16. Maurice Merleau-Ponty, *The Visible and the Invisible*, 155.
17. de Man, *Allegories of Reading*, 49.

18. Wodtke, "Das Problem," 97.
19. ". . . you, still almost a child, complete / for an instant the dance-figure / into the sheer constellation of one of those dances / wherein we transiently surpass // nature's dull ordering . . ." *Sonnets*, II:28, *Werke*, I, 769f.
20. de Man, *Allegories of Reading*, 32, 37.
21. Ibid., 31.
22. Ibid., 49.
23. "That projective spirit which masters all things earthly / loves, in the figure's sweep, nothing but the turning point." *Sonnets*, II:12, *Werke*, I, 758.
24. ". . . while you see it, the lightly reserved / midst of the cashmere shawl which, out of the space of flowers, / renews itself in blackness, clarifies itself from out of the border's edges, / and which creates a pure space for space . . .: / you experience this: that names are / endlessly wasted on it: for it is the midst. / However this may be, the pattern for our steps; / around such an emptiness we revolve." "Shawl," *Werke*, II 477. For a discussion, see Beda Allemann, *Zeit und Figur beim späten Rilke* (Pfullingen: Neske, 1961), 96–115.
25. "Yet, may it delight us now for a while / to trust the figure. That is enough." *Sonnets*, I:11, *Werke*, I, 737.
26. Cf. M. Heidegger's late Zähringen seminar in *Vier Seminare*, with translations from the French by Curd Ochwadt (Frankfurt a. M.: Klostermann, 1977), 133ff, for a last discussion of this Parmenidean metaphor.
27. "King's heart. Core of a high / rulership, Balsam fruit. / Golden heart-nut. / Urn's poppy / in the midst of the middle structure / (where the echo is refracted, / like a splinter of stillness, / when you stir, / because it seems to you / that your prior demeanor was too loud . . .) / [You,] withdrawn from peoples, / star-minded, / in invisible circles / circling, king's heart. // Where is, whereto / that of the light / favorite? / : smile, from without / laid upon gay fruit's / hesitant roundness / perhaps, or upon the moth's / preciousness, crape-wings, antennae. // Where, however, where, that which sang them, / which sang them into one, / the poet's heart? / :Wind, / invisible, / wind's inner." "Mausoleum," *Werke*, II, 500f.
28. Gerald L. Bruns, *Heidegger's Estrangements: Language, Truth, and Poetry in the Later Writings* (New Haven and London: Yale University Press, 1988).

CHAPTER 4. TEXTUALITY AND THE QUESTION OF ORIGIN: HEIDEGGER'S READING OF 'ANDENKEN' AND 'DER ISTER'

1. Cited by F.-W. v. Hermann in his "Postscript" to M. Heidegger, *Erläuterungen zu Hölderlins Dichtung*, GA 4. See also Beda Allemann's discussion of Heidegger's letter in *Hölderlin und Heidegger*; "Zürcher Beiträge zur deutschen Literatur- und Geistesgeschichte," vol. 6, Emil Staiger, ed. (Zurich: Atlantis, 1954), 7ff.
2. M. Heidegger, *Hölderlins Hymne "Der Ister"*; Freiburger Vorlesung, Sommersemester 1942, GA 53 (1984), 2.
3. Annemarie Gethmann-Siefert, "Heidegger and Hölderlin: The Over-Usage of 'Poets in an Impoverished Time'," Richard Taft, trans., *Research in Phenomenology*, XIX (1989), 59–88 (63).
4. See M. Heidegger, *Einführung in die Metaphysik*, 152.
5. Rodolphe Gasché, "Introduction" to Andrzej Warminski, *Readings in Interpretation: Hölderlin, Hegel, Heidegger*, History and Theory of Literature,

vol. 26 (Minneapolis: University of Minnesota Press, 1987), ix–xxvi (xv).

6. For Heidegger's statement, see "Wie wenn am Feiertage ..." GA 4, 51.

7. Gasché, "Introduction" to *Readings in Interpretation*, xv.

8. Compare here "Only a God Can Save Us," 62.

9. *Hölderlin und Heidegger*, 38–43. As Allemann points out, Heidegger follows a strand of Hölderlin scholarship derived from Beissner, Michel, and Hellingrath in interpreting the turning so as to give priority to the Greek/Hesperian relationship.

10. "For they wanted to found / a reign of art. Therewith, however / that which pertained to their homeland was / neglected by them; and miserably / Greece, the most beautiful, perished." *Stuttgarter Hölderlin Ausgabe*, Friedrich Beissner, ed. (Stuttgart: Kohlhammer, 1949–1957), II, 228. Cited as SA.

11. M. Heidegger, "Der Ursprung des Kunstwerkes," *Holzwege*, GA 5, 1–74. English translation by Albert Hofstadter, "The Origin of the Work of Art," PLT, 15–87.

12. "Only a God Can Save Us," 61.

13. M. Heidegger, *Parmenides (Wintersemester 1942/43)*, GA 54.

14. Gethmann-Siefert, "Heidegger and Hölderlin," 70.

15. Ibid. Compare Heidegger's explicit conflation in "The Origin of the Work of Art," GA 5, 49; PLT, 61f.

16. See Derrida, *De l'esprit*, passim.

17. Christopher Fynsk, "Finitude de la *Dichtung*," in *Hölderlin*, Jean-François Courtine, ed., "Cahiers de l'Herne" (Paris: Editions de l'Herne, 1989), 444–456 (454).

18. *Hölderlin to Böhlendorff*, 4 December 1801, and 2 December 1802, SA V, 318ff, 327ff. Cited GA 4, 82; GA 52, 22f.

19. GA 53, 157. Derrida fails to take notice of this passage when he writes, at the outset of *De l'esprit*, ch. iii, that, "to my knowledge, Heidegger never asked himself, 'What is spirit?'" (31).

20. "We, however, sing from the Indus / come from afar / and from the Alpheus ... // I suppose he would have to come / from the East. / Much could be / said about this ..." (SA II, 191).

21. In reworking an earlier version, Hölderlin changed "nach Indien" to "zu Indiern." Jean-Pierre Lefebvre interprets the destination as the West Indies in "Auch die Stege sind Holzwege. Interprétation de *Andenken*," Bernhard Böschenstein and Jacques le Rider, ed., *Hölderlin vu de France* (Tübingen: Günter Narr, 1987), 53–76.

22. Jean-François Marquet, "Structure de la mythologie hölderlinienne," in Courtine, ed., *Hölderlin*, 352–369.

23. "... But how? A sign is needed / nothing else, as well may be, so that sun / and moon it may carry in its soul, inseparable, / and move on, day and night as well ..." (SA II, 191).

24. "Structure de la mythologie," 353.

25. "Not good is it, / to be soulless of mortal / thoughts. But good / is a conversation ..." (SA II, 189).

26. Whereas Heidegger seems unaware of the second reading, Lefebvre appears to favor it in his translation of the poem; for he writes "De perdre l'âme à coup de mortelles / Pensées ..." See Courtine, ed., *Hölderlin*, 26f. For an English translation, see Richard Sieburth, *Hölderlin; Hymns and Fragments* (Princeton: Princeton University Press, 1984).

27. See here Heidegger's 1967 essay, "Die Herkunft der Kunst und die Bestimmung des Denkens," and "Die Frage nach der Technik."
28. GA 5, 62; PLT, 74.
29. Jean-Luc Nancy, "La joie d'Hypérion," in Courtine, ed., *Hölderlin*, 200–216 (202).
30. Nancy, "La joie d'Hypérion," 206.
31. GA 4, 146f. See also Jacques Derrida, "Qual Quelle; Valéry's Sources," trans. Alan Bass, *Margins of Philosophy* (Chicago: University of Chicago Press, 1982), 273–306.
32. "Finitude de la *Dichtung*," 444. The reference is to Hölderlin's "In lieblicher Bläue . . ." SA II, 373.

CHAPTER 5. MNEMOSYNE'S DEATH AND THE FAILURE OF MOURNING

1. See Heidegger, *Hölderlins Hymne "Andenken,"* GA 52, 3.
2. GA 52, 103. Compare also Heidegger's discussion of evil in "Die Sprache im Gedicht," *Unterwegs zur Sprache*, 60, as well as "Vom Wesen der Wahrheit," *Wegmarken*, 73–97. English translations, "Language in the Poem" (see ch. ii, note 4), and "On the Essence of Truth," John Sallis, trans., BW, 117–141.
3. Heidegger, "Die Frage nach der Technik," 5–36 (26).
4. For a discussion of ambiguity in Heidegger, see the concluding pages of Véronique M. Fóti, "Politics at the Limit of Metaphysics: Heidegger, Ferry & Renaut, and Lyotard," *The Graduate Faculty Philosophy Journal*, special issue on "Heidegger and the Political," forthcoming, 1991.
5. Apart from GA 52, see also "Andenken," GA 4, 79–152.
6. Anselm Haverkamp, "Error in Mourning—A Crux in Hölderlin: 'dem gleich fehlet die Trauer' ('Mnemosyne')," Vernon Chadwick, trans., *The Lesson of Paul de Man*, "Yale French Studies," 69 (New Haven and London: Yale University Press, 1985), 238–253 (246).
7. The "Andenken" lecture course of 1941/42 was to include a discussion of "Mnemosyne," as did the lecture course on Hölderlin's Ister hymn, which Heidegger gave the following semester (GA, 53). Heidegger's 1968 essay "Das Gedicht" (GA 4, 182–192) refers repeatedly to "Mnemosyne" but skirts a fuller discussion. See also ". . . Dichterisch wohnet der Mensch . . .," *Vorträge und Aufsätze*, II 61–78, and *Einführung in die Metaphysik*, 75–88. ". . . Dichterisch wohnet der Mensch . . ." appears in the English translation of Albert Hofstadter, ". . . Poetically Man Dwells . . ." in PLT, 211–229.
8. Allemann, *Hölderlin und Heidegger*.
9. GA 52, 54. See Heidegger, "Hölderlins Hymne 'Der Ister'," GA 53.
10. Allemann, *Hölderlin und Heidegger*, 131.
11. GA 52, 110–125. See Pindar, *Pythia* VIII, 95f.
12. Cf. Heidegger, *Parmenides*, GA 54, passim.
13. Friedrich Hölderlin, "Das Werden im Vergehen," *Stuttgarter Hölderlin Ausgabe*, IV, 282–287; Pfau, 96–100.
14. Michel Haar, "Heidegger and the God of Hölderlin," *Research in Phenomenology*, XIX (1989), 89–100.
15. Jacques Derrida, "The Politics of Friendship," *The Journal of Philosophy*, 85:11 (November 1988), 632–649.

16. GA 52, 170. See also Heidegger, "Der Ursprung des Kunstwerkes," GA 5, 49.
17. Derrida, "The Politics of Friendship," 644.
18. Jürgen Habermas, "Work and *Weltanschauung*: The Heidegger Controversy from a German Perspective," John McCumber, trans., in Arnold I. Davidson, ed., "Symposium on Heidegger and Nazism," *Critical Inquiry*, 15:2 (Winter, 1989), 431–456 (440).
19. Habermas, "Work and *Weltanschauung*," 441.
20. Heidegger, "Only a God Can Save Us," 62. See also Heidegger, *Einführung in die Metaphysik*, 43.
21. Besides Heidegger, "The Self-Assertion of the German University," see also his "German Students" (3 November 1933); "German Men and Women" (10 November 1933); and "Declaration of Support for Adolf Hitler" (11 November 1933) concerning his adulation of the *Führer*. These texts are reprinted in Richard Wolin, "Martin Heidegger and Politics: a Dossier," *New German Critique*, 55 (Fall, 1988), 101–104.
22. Habermas, "Work and *Weltanschauung*," 447.
23. Philippe Lacoue-Labarthe, "La césure du spéculatif," *L'imitation des modernes; typographies II* (Paris: Galilée, 1986), 41.
24. ". . . And much / as upon the shoulders a / load of firewood is // to be retained . . ." Hölderlin, "Mnemosyne" (third version), in *Sämtliche Werke*, Historical-Critical Edition, D. E. Sattler, ed. (Frankfurt a. M.: Stroemfeld/Roter Stern, 1976–1988), vol. 2, 193–198. This "Frankfurt Edition" will be referred to as FA.
25. Lacoue-Labarthe, *Heidegger, Art and Politics*, 42. For in-text references, this work will be cited as HAP.
26. Haverkamp, "Error in Mourning," 250.
27. Haverkamp/Chadwick translate "es ereignet sich aber / Das Wahre" as "what is true is bound to take place" ("Error in Mourning," 250). Given that (a) *sich ereignen* carries no connotation of compulsion and (b) Hölderlin is Heidegger's rival in attending to the etymological meanings of words, this translation is questionable.
28. Haverkamp, "Error in Mourning," 250.
29. ". . . and there trill / lost in the air the larks and under the day there pasture / well-herded the sheep of heaven" ("Mnemosyne," I, v.24f; II, v.23f.).
    ". . . for good are / if with contrary speech the soul / has wounded [been wounded by] / A heavenly one, the signs of day" ("Mnemosyne," II, v.22–24).
30. See Jochen Schmidt, "Der Begriff des Zorns in Hölderlins Spätwerk," *Hölderlin Jahrbuch*, 15 (1967–68), 128–157.
31. "For snow, like the flowers of May / signifying the noble-spirited, wherever / it may be, gleams upon / the green meadow / of the alps, halved . . ."
32. English translation by Thomas Pfau, *Friedrich Hölderlin: Essays and Letters on Theory* (Albany: SUNY Press, 1988), 111.
33. Klaus Düsing, "Die Theorie der Tragödie bei Hölderlin und Hegel," Christoph Jamme and Otto Pöggeler, ed., *Jenseits des Idealismus: Hölderlins letzte Homburger Jahre (1804–1806)* (Bonn: Bouvier, 1988), 55–82 (61).
34. Pfau, *Essays and Letters*, 115.
35. Allemann, *Hölderlin und Heidegger*, 156f.
36. Friedrich Beissner, "Erläuterungen," SA 2, 828; and F. Beissner, "Hölderlins letzte Hymne," *Hölderlin Jahrbuch* (1948–49), 66–102.
37. "By the figtree my / Achilles died (to me)."

38. See Beissner, "Erläuterungen," SA 2, 828, and *Iliad*, 6, 433; 11, 167; 22, 145; also Matthew 24, 32; Mark 13, 28; Luke 21, 29.
39. Peter Szondi, "Gattungspoetik und Geschichtsphilosophie," *Hölderlin-Studien* (Frankfurt: Suhrkamp, 1967–70), 146.
40. Haverkamp, "Error in Mourning," 242.
41. Haverkamp comments on Beissner's discovery that the trope of severing the lock of hair in "Mnemosyne" mirrors Schiller's "Dido," which also dates from 1803 ("Error in Mourning," 244).
42. If *gleich* is read as a temporal indicator, the verses can be read as "to that one / right away mourning is lacking." Such a reading, however, has little to recommend it. On the model of v. 103 of "Der Einzige" ("Dem gleich ist gefangen die Seele der Helden"), *gleich* is better construed as a comparative, yielding "Like unto that one, mourning fails."

   It is interesting that Paul de Man stops just short of reading the last two verses in his two essays that address "Mnemosyne," "The Image of Rousseau in the Poetry of Hölderlin" and "Wordsworth and Hölderlin," in *The Rhetoric of Romanticism* (New York: Columbia University Press, 1984), 19–45, 47–65.
43. Jochen Schmidt, in *Hölderlins letzte Hymnen* (Tübingen: Niemeyer, 1970), finds that both poet and hero engage in a mournful (nostalgic) commemoration which fails to bring about a meaningful life-integration, whereas Beissner, in his "Erläuterungen," writes that the mourner shows the same fault or failing as the one who, in an excess of feeling, gives himself over to death without resistance (830).
44. Haverkamp, "Error in Mourning," 290.
45. For a discussion of Hegel's theory of tragedy, see Düsing, "Die Theorie der Tragödie," as well as Peter Szondi, "The Notion of the Tragic in Schelling, Hölderlin, and Hegel," *On Textual Understanding and Other Essays*, Harvey Mendelsohn, trans.; "Theory and History of Literature," vol. 15 (Minneapolis: University of Minnesota Press, 1986), 43–55. See also Otto Pöggeler, "Hegel und die griechische Tragödie," *Hegel-Studien*, Beiheft 1 (1964), 285–305.
46. Düsing, "Die Theorie der Tragödie," 79.
47. Pfau, *Essays and Letters*, 108.
48. Emmanuel Levinas, *Time and the Other*, Richard A. Cohen, trans. (Pittsburgh: Duquesne University Press, 1987), 69, 80.
49. Lacoue-Labarthe, HAP, 44.
50. Hölderlin, "Anmerkungen zum Ödipus," FA 16, 249–258 (257). Translation by Pfau, *Essays and Letters*, 101–108.

   According to D. E. Sattler's note, the text which Hölderlin refers to translates as follows: "That Aristotle was the scribe of nature, immersing his pen in sense." Hölderlin, however, leaves out the reference to Aristotle and alters the text. Since the modified statement must be read in context, I translate the entire paragraph:

   > The presentation (*Darstellung*) of tragedy rests above all on this, that the monstrous—how God and man are coupled and [how], without limits, the power of nature and man's inmost become one in wrath—grasps itself in that the limitless unification is purified by limitless separation. "Nature's scribe dips his well-minded pen."
51. Allemann, *Hölderlin und Heidegger*, 166.
52. Lacoue-Labarthe, "La césure du spéculatif," 43.
53. See Heidegger's infamous statements assimilating "the manufacture of corpses in

gas chambers" to mechanized food industry and the manufacture of hydrogen bombs, and characterizing the victims of genocide as "disponible components of a disponible resource in the manufacture of corpses," in his 1949 lectures "Das Ge-stell" ("Posure") and "Die Gefahr" ("The Danger"). For discussion, see Thomas Sheehan, "Heidegger and the Nazis," *New York Review of Books,* 16 June 1988, 38–47; Lacoue-Labarthe, *Heidegger, Art and Politics,* ch. 5; and Véronique M. Fóti, "Politics at the Limit of Metaphysics: Heidegger, Ferry & Renaut, and Lyotard."

54. Maurice Blanchot, *The Writing of the Disaster,* Ann Smock, trans. (Lincoln and London: University of Nebraska Press, 1986).

55. Edmond Jabès, *From the Desert to the Book; Dialogues with Marcel Cohen,* Pierre Joris, trans. (Barrytown, N.Y.: Station Hill Press, 1990), 62.

56. See Cyrus Hamlin's discussion of Adorno's term "Fügsamkeit," Böschenstein-Schäfer's "Demut," and Benjamin's thematization of Hölderlin's "Blödigkeit" in "'Stimmen des Geschiks': The Hermeneutics of Unreadability. (Thoughts on Hölderlin's 'Griechenland')," *Jenseits des Idealismus,* 252–276 (266).

57. Allemann, *Hölderlin und Heidegger,* 166–170. See also Bernhard Böschenstein, "Hölderlins späteste Gedichte," in Jochen Scmidt, ed., *Über Hölderlin* (Frankfurt a. M.: Insel Verlag, 1970), 153–174.

58. Heidegger, "Hölderlins Erde und Himmel," *Erläuterungen zu Hölderlins Dichtung,* GA 4, 152–181. For the poem, see FA 9, 191f.

59. Hamlin, "Stimmen des Geschiks," 266.

60. Whereas Beissner, in SA, organizes the text into three distinct "versions," Sattler, in FA, superimposes these to yield a "reconstructed text." For a discussion, see Hamlin, "Stimmen des Geschiks."

61. Theodor W. Adorno, "Parataxis—zur späten Lyrik Hölderlins," *Noten zur Literatur 3* (Frankfurt a. M.: Suhrkamp, 1965), 156–204.

62. As cited by Heidegger from Valéry's open letter "La crise de l'esprit" (1919), in "Hölderlins Erde und Himmel," 176.

63. Renate Böschenstein-Schäfer, "Die Sprache des Zeichens in Hölderlins hymnischen Fragmenten," *Hölderlin Jahrbuch,* 19/20 (1975/77), 267–284. See also her retrospective comments on this essay in "Hölderlins allegorische Ausdrucksform," *Jenseits des Idealismus,* 181–209.

64. Since I am not as persuaded as Hamlin of the utter unreadability of the poem, even after the hermeneutic problems concerning the manuscript are acknowledged, I venture the following translation. May the reader bear its necessarily interpretive character in mind.

"... Where thereupon / Resounding like the calf's skin / The earth, out of devastation, temptations of the saints— / For initially the work takes form— / Follows great laws[;] the sciences and tenderness[,] and the sky vast of pure raiment[,] thereafter / Appearing[,] sing clouds of song. / For firm is the earth's / navel. Captive namely in shores of grass are / The flames and the universal / Elements. But pure of mind there lives the ether above. But silver / On pure days / Is the light. As a sign of love / Violet-blue the earth." Hölderlin, "Griechenland," III, v. 9–22, SA 2, 257.

Richard Sieburth's translation, in *Hölderlin's Hymns and Fragments* (Princeton: Princeton University Press, 1985), 207, follows Sattler's reconstructed text, which synthesizes the three "versions."

CHAPTER 6. A MISSED INTERLOCUTION: HEIDEGGER AND CELAN

1. At the time of this meeting, Heidegger was seventy-eight, Celan forty-seven years old. The second meeting took place shortly before Celan's death in 1970. Apart from these personal meetings, there was also at least one meeting in a professional context, as documented by Gerhardt Baumann in *Erinnerungen an Paul Celan* (Frankfurt a. M.: Suhrkamp, 1986).
2. This silence has been criticized, in particular, by Maurice Blanchot. See, for instance, "Thinking the Apocalypse; a Letter from Maurice Blanchot to Catherine Davis," Paula Wissig, trans., in Arnold I. Davidson, ed., "Symposium on Heidegger and Nazism," 475–480.
3. Sieghild Bogumil, "Todtnauberg," Hans-Michael Speier, ed., *Celan-Jahrbuch 2* (1988), 37–51 (39).
4. Werner Hamacher, "The Second of Inversion: Movements of a Figure through Celan's Poetry," William D. Jewett, trans., in *The Lesson of Paul de Man*, 276–311; and Evelyn Hünneke, "Hoffnung auf ein menschliches Heute und Morgen: Zur Wirklichkeit in der Dichtung Paul Celans," *Celan-Jahrbuch 1* (1987), 141–171.
5. Heidegger, "Only a God Can Save Us," 53.
6. See Jean-François Lyotard, *Heidegger et "les juifs"* (Paris: Galilée, 1988).
7. "Arnica, eyebright, / the / draught from the well with the / star-die upon it, // in the / hut, // written into the book / —whose name did it receive / before mine?—, / written into the book / the line about / a hope, today, for a thinking one's / coming / word / in the heart, // woodland swards, unlevelled, / orchid and orchid, singly, // crude things, later, in driving, / distinct, // he who drives us, the man, / who listens in, // the half- / trodden rod- / paths in the high moor, // of the moist, / much" PC II, 255.
8. Heidegger, "Why Do I Stay in the Provinces? (1934)," trans. Thomas Sheehan, in *Heidegger: the Man and the Thinker*, 27–29.
9. See Otto Pöggeler, *Spur des Worts; zur Lyrik Paul Celans* (Freiburg/Munich: Karl Alber, 1986), 266.
10. "Why Do I Stay in the Provinces?," 28.
11. See "Wozu Dichter?," GA 5, 271; PLT, 93.
12. Maurice Blanchot, *The Unavowable Community*, trans. Pierre Joris (Barrytown, N.Y.: Station Hill Press, 1988).
13. Heidegger, "Aus einem Gespräch von der Sprache," GA 12, 115; *On the Way to Language*, 29.
14. "Die Sprache im Gedicht," GA 12, 34; *On the Way to Language*, 160.
15. "I drink wine from two glasses / and plough ahead on / the kingly caesura / like That One / on Pindar, // God relinquishes the tuning fork / as one of the small / just ones, // out of the lottery drum falls / our whit" (PC III, 108). (Note: while *Deut* means an insignificant share or portion, it also connotes *Deutung* or interpretation.)
16. Hölderlin, "Anmerkungen zum Ödipus," FA 14, 205; Pfau, 102.
17. As a colloquial term, *zackern* means "to plough"; it carries the connotation of oscillating or moving in a zig-zag pattern.
18. For a discussion of Celan's relationship to Jewish mysticism, see Pöggeler, *Spur des Worts*, Pt. B, ch. 2, and passim.
19. PC I, 251f. Pöggeler discusses this poem and its allusions to Baudelaire and Hoffmansthal extensively in *Spur des Worts*. See especially "Der schärfere Pfeil," 300–334.

20. See Heidegger, "Logos," *Vorträge und Aufsätze*, III, 5–25; *Early Greek Thinking*, 57–78.
21. Cf. Paul Celan, "Der Meridian," PC III, 187–202, and the discussion in chapter 7, below.
22. Alan Udoff, "On Poetic Dwelling: Situating Celan and the Holocaust," in Amy D. Colin, ed., *Argumentum e Silentio; International Celan Symposium* (Berlin: De Gruyter, 1987), 320–351.
23. Lacoue-Labarthe, *Heidegger, Art and Politics*, 46.
24. PC 1, 195–204. See Peter Szondi, "Durch die Enge geführt," *Celan-Studien* (Frankfurt a. M.: Suhrkamp, 1972), 47–11. English translation by D. Caldwell and S. Esh, "Reading, 'Engführung': An Essay on the Poetry of Paul Celan," *Boundary 2* XI:3 (Spring, 1983), 231–264.
25. See Peter Szondi, "The Poetry of Constancy: Paul Celan's Translation of Shakespeare's Sonnet 105," in P. Szondi, *On Textual Understanding, and Other Essays*, Harvey Mendelsohn, trans. (Minneapolis: University of Minnesota Press, 1986), 161–178. The fugue is defined in "Reading 'Engführung'," 236.
26. Caldwell and Esh, "Reading 'Engführung'," 236.
27. Sieghild Bogumil, "Celans Hölderlinlektüre im Gegenlicht des schlichten Wortes," *Celan-Jahrbuch 1*, 81–125 (85).
28. "Deported into the / terrain / with the undeceiving trace: // Grass, written asunder. The stones, white, / with the shadows of grass-blades: / Read no longer—look! / Look no longer—go! // Go, your hour / has no sisters, you are— / are at home. A wheel, slowly, / rolls out of itself, the spokes / climb upon a blackish field, the night / needs no stars, nowhere / are you being asked for."
29. Caldwell and Esh, "Reading 'Engführung'," 232.
30. "Nowhere / are you being asked for—The place where they lay, it has / a name—it has / none. They did not lie there. Something / lay between them. They / did not see through. // Did not see, no, / talked about / words. None / awoke, / sleep / came over them."
31. Stefan George, "Das Wort." See Heidegger, "Das Wesen der Sprache," and "Das Wort," GA 12, 145–225; *On the Way to Language*, 57–108; 139–156. For further discussion of George's poetry, see H.-G. Gadamer, *Poetica* (Zurich: Insel Verlag, 1977), 7–76.
32. Heidegger, "Das Wort." For a discussion, see Robert Bernasconi, *The Question of Language in Heidegger's History of Being* (Atlantic Highlands, N.J.: Humanities Press, 1985), ch. 4.
33. "Came, came. Nowhere / asked for—It is I, I, / I lay between you, I was / open, was / audible, I ticked at you, your breath / obeyed, it is / I still, but you / are sleeping."
34. Caldwell and Esh, "Reading 'Engführung'," 240.
35. "Is I still—Years. / Years, years, a finger / feels downward and closer, feels / about: / sutures, palpable, here / it gapes wide open, there / it grew together again—who / covered it up?"
36. "Covered it / over—who? Came, came. Came a word, came, / came through the night, / wanted to shine, wanted to shine. // Ash. / Ash, ash. / Night. / Night-and-night.—To / the eye go, the moist one."
37. H.-G. Gadamer, "Celans Schlussgedicht," *Argumentum e Silentio*, 58–71 (71).
38. "To / the eye go, / to the moist one—Whirlwinds. / Whirlwinds, since ever, / flurries of particles, the other, / you / know it, we / read it in the book, was / opinion. // Was, was / opinion. How / did we grasp each other / grasp—with /

these / hands? // It also stood written, that. / Where? We / put a silence over it, / poison-stilled, great, / one green / silence, a sepal, there / hung on it a thought of the plant-like— / green, yes, / hung, yes, / under a sneering / sky. // Of, yes, / the plantlike."

39. Philippe Forget, "Neuere Daten über Paul Celan," *Celan-Jahrbuch 1*, 217–222.
40. GA 12, 250; *On the Way to Language*, 130.
41. "Yes, / whirlwinds, par- / ticle-flurries, / there remained / time, remained, / to try it out with the stone—it [he] / was hospitable, it [he] / did not interrupt. How / good we had it. // Grainy, / grainy and fibrous. Stalkish, / dense [poetize!]: / grapish and ray-like; kidneyish, / plate-like and / cloddish; loose, many- / branched—: he, it / did not interrupt, it / spoke, / spoke gladly to dry eyes, ere it closed them. // Spoke, spoke. / Was, was. // We / did not desist, stood / in the midst, one / pore-structure, and / it came. // Came towards us, came / through, mended / invisibly, mended / at the last membrane, / and / the world, a thousand-crystal, / took form, took form."
42. Werner Hamacher, "The Second of Inversion: Movements of a Figure through a Celan's Poetry," William D. Jewett, trans., *The Lesson of Paul de Man*, 276–311.
43. "Took form, took form. / Then— // Nights, demixed. Circles, / red or blue, red / squares: the / world pledged its inmost / in play with the new / hours—Circles, / red or black, bright / squares, no / flight's shadow, no / planetable, no / smoke-soul mounts and joins in.
44. See Hugo Huppert, "'Spirituell'. Ein Gespräch mit Paul Celan," in W. Hamacher and W. Menninghaus, eds., *Paul Celan* (Frankfurt: Suhrkamp, 1988), 319–324.
45. H.-G. Gadamer, "Philosophy and Poetry," in Robert Bernasconi, ed., *The Relevance of the Beautiful, and Other Essays*, trans. Nicholas Walker (Cambridge: Cambridge University Press, 1986), 132.
46. Mounts and / joins in—At the owls' flight, by / the petrified leprosy, / by / our fled hands, in / the youngest outcasting, / over the butts on / the buried wall: // visible, a- / new: the channels, the // choirs, at that time, the / psalms. Ho-, ho- / sanna. // So / there still stand temples. One / star / may still have light. / Nothing, / nothing is lost. // Ho- / sanna. // At the owl's flight, here, / the conversations, day-gray, / of groundwater-traces."
47. Caldwell and Esh, "Reading 'Engführung'," 256.
48. "(—day-gray, / of / groundwater-traces—Deported / into the terrain / with / the undeceiving / trace: // Grass, / grass, / written asunder.)
49. Udoff, "Poetic Dwelling," 321. Udoff's essay is also valuable for its discussion of midrashic thinking.
50. Stéphane Mallarmé, "Crise de vers," *Oeuvres complètes* (Paris, 1945), 306. Cited by Szondi in "Reading 'Engführung'."
51. Huppert, "Spirituell," 321.
52. Celan's comments refer to his poem "Sprachgitter" and are quoted by Huppert, "Spirituell," 320.
53. Bernasconi, *The Question of Language*, 46f.
54. GA 12, 181f.; *On the Way to Language*, 87f.
55. Heidegger, "Das Ge-stell," which is the first (unpublished) version of "The Question Concerning Technology." The published version deletes most of this statement. For quotations from Heidegger's typescripts, see Wolfgang Schirmacher, *Technik und Gelassenheit* (Freiburg: Karl Alber, 1983). For discussion, see Thomas Sheehan, "Heidegger and the Nazis," *New York Review of Books*,

16 June 1988, 38–47 (42), and Véronique M. Fóti, "Politics at the Limit of Metaphysics: Heidegger, Ferry & Renaut, and Lyotard."

CHAPTER 7. MERIDIANS OF ENCOUNTER

1. PC III, 187–202.
2. Pöggeler, *Spur des Worts*, 12. Pöggeler points out that the drafts are extant.
3. Pöggeler, *Spur des Worts*, 13, 47.
4. Lacoue-Labarthe, *La poésie comme expérience* (Paris: Bourgeois, 1986).
5. Jacques Derrida, *Shibboleth; pour Paul Celan* (Paris: Galilée, 1986).
6. Lacoue-Labarthe, *Heidegger, Art and Politics*, ch. 7.
7. PC III, 188. The reference is to Büchner's play *Leonce and Lena*.
8. Heidegger, "Die Frage nach der Technik," 35; "The Question Concerning Technology," 317.
9. Pöggeler points out these connections, *Spur des Worts*, 145. For a discussion of political references in "Der Meridian," see Christoph Jamme, "'Unserer Daten eingedenk'; Paul Celans 'Der Meridian' in der Diskussion," in Annemarie Gethmann-Siefert, ed., *Philosophie und Poesie*, vol. 2 (Stuttgart-Bad Cannstatt: Fromann-Holzbog Verlag, 1988), 281–308. This article constitutes an excellent review of recent interpretive literature.
10. Derrida, *Shibboleth*, 47.
11. Ibid., 48.
12. Ibid., 40.
13. See Derrida, "Freud and the Scene of Writing," in *Writing and Difference*, Alan Bass, trans. (Chicago: University of Chicago Press, 1978), 196–231.
14. For a discussion, see Philippe Forget, "Neuere Daten über Paul Celan," 217–222.
15. Derrida, *Shibboleth*, 17.
16. Emmanuel Levinas, *Ethics and Infinity; Conversations with Philippe Nemo*, Richard A. Cohen, trans. (Pittsburgh: Duquesne University Press, 1985), 105.
17. See Gadamer's essay, "Verstummen die Dichter?," in *Poetica*, 103–118.
18. Derrida, *Shibboleth*, 32.
19. See Bernhard Böschenstein, "Celan und Mandelstamm," *Celan-Jahrbuch 2*, 155–158 (156).
20. This letter is cited by Pöggeler, *Spur des Worts*, 162, and by Evelyn Hünneke, "Hoffnung auf ein menschliches Heute und Morgen. Zur Wirklichkeit in der Dichtung Paul Celans," *Celan-Jahrbuch 1*, 141–171 (168).
21. Ibid.
22. Ibid.
23. Ibid. It is perhaps significant that, in Kepler's time, no technique for projecting the meridian had yet been developed. There is hence a certain "uninterpretability" in the concept. Other illusions in Celan's letter are to Plato's *Phaedrus*, and possibly to crystallography (a frequent reference in Celan), where the concept of the pole carries a technical meaning. It denotes the point of intersection between a straight line perpendicular to a plane of the crystal and the ideal sphere of projection. Celan appears to be suggesting an inversion which gives priority to the projection (the ideal) over what is projected, thus to the ideal sphere over the planes.
24. Ibid.

25. "Great / goes the banished one up there, the / burned one, a Pomeranian, at home / in the junebug-song, which remained motherly, light- / blossoming at the edge / of all harsh / winter-hard cold / syllables. // With him / wander the meridians: / ad- / sorbed by his / sun-steered pain, which fraternally links countries, in accordance / with the noonday saying of a / loving / distance . . ." (PC I, 287–291).

    In the first of the two strophes, the references are to the German children's song "Maikäfer flieg . . ." I have translated *Maikäfer* as "junebug" rather than as "cockchafer" because the former term has much the same literal meaning and connotations as the German one, even if it may not be entomologically quite correct.

26. See Heidegger, *Hölderlins Hymne "Der Ister,"* GA 53, 99–108; and *Parmenides*, GA 54, 132ff.

27. "Die Pole . . ." (PC III, 105). This poem forms part of the posthumous collection *Zeitgehöft*.

POSTSCRIPT

1. Silvia Benso, "Con Heidegger. Contro Heidegger. Suggestioni per un'etica ontologica," *Filosofia e Teologia*, 2 (1991), forthcoming. I cite from an English-language version which the author is preparing for publication.

2. Schürmann, *Heidegger on Being and Acting*, 287f.

Selective Bibliography

◆

This bibliography includes only titles significant for the writing of the present book. No attempt is made to list the complete writings of any author (including Heidegger) or to document fully the literature on any relevant issue.

HEIDEGGER: TEXTS

Most references to Heidegger's works are to the *Gesamtausgabe (Collected Works)*, still in the process of publication by Vittorio Klostermann, Frankfurt a. M. For current listings of published volumes and translations (French and English), consult the ongoing bibliography in *Heidegger Studies*. Key works such as *Sein und Zeit*, *Holzwege*, *Wegmarken* and *Unterwegs zur Sprache* are also sometimes referred to in the older editions, which are more readily available. See Notes, above.

GA 1:   *Sein und Zeit*. Ed. Friedrich-Wilhelm von Herrmann. 1977.

GA 4:   *Erläuterungen zu Hölderlins Dichtung*. Ed. Friedrich-Wilhelm von Hermann. 1982.

GA 5:   *Holzwege*. Ed. Friedrich-Wilhelm von Hermann. 1977.

GA 9:   *Wegmarken*. Ed. Friedrich-Wilhelm von Hermann. 1976.

GA 12:   *Unterwegs zur Sprache*. Ed. Friedrich-Wilhelm von Hermann. 1985.

GA 13:   *Aus der Erfahrung des Denkens*. Ed. Hermann Heidegger. 1983.

GA 39:   *Hölderlins Hymnen "Germanien" und "Der Rhein"* (Wintersemester 1934/35). Ed. Susanne Ziegler. 1980.

GA 40:   *Einführung in die Metaphysik* (Sommersemester 1935). Ed. Petra Jaeger. 1983.

GA 43:   *Nietzsche: Der Wille zur Macht als Kunst* (Wintersemester 1936/37). Ed. Bernd Heimbuchel. 1985.

GA 52:   *Hölderlins Hymne "Andenken"* (Wintersemester 1941/42). Ed. Curd Ochwadt. 1982.

GA 53:   *Hölderlins Hymne "Der Ister."* Ed. Walter Biemel. 1984.

GA 54:   *Parmenides* (Wintersemester 1942/43). Ed. Manfred S. Frings. 1982.

GA 55:   *Heraklit*. 1: *Der Anfang des abendländischen Denkens (Heraklit)* (Sommersemester 1943). 2: *Logik. Heraklits Lehre vom Logos* (Sommersemester 1944). Ed. Manfred S. Frings. 1979.

GA 65:   *Beiträge zur Philosophie. (Vom Ereignis)* Ed. Friedrich-Wilhelm von Hermann. 1989.

Heidegger: Other Texts

For English translations and for references to the typescript and the French translation of an essay by Heidegger not published in German or English, please consult Notes, above.

Die Selbstbehauptung der deutschen Universität. Das Rektorat 1933/34: Tatsachen und Gedanken. Ed. Hermann Heidegger. Frankfurt a. M.: Klostermann, 1983.

Die Technik und die Kehre. Pfullingen: Neske, 1962.

Gelassenheit. 2nd ed. Pfullingen: Neske, 1960.

Identität und Differenz. 7th ed. Pfullingen: Neske, 1982.

Vorträge und Aufsätze. 3 vols. 3rd ed. Pfullingen: Neske, 1967.

Was heisst Denken? Tübingen: Niemeyer, 1954.

THE POETS: TEXTS AND TRANSLATIONS

Paul Celan

Gessamelte Werke. 5 vols. Ed. Beda Allemann and Stefan Reichert. Frankfurt a. M.: Suhrkamp, 1983.

Paul Celan: Poems. Trans. Michael Hamburger. Manchester: Carcanet New Press, Ltd., 1980.

"Poems by Paul Celan." Trans. Michael Hamburger. *Temenos*, 6 (1985), 46–56.

Paul Celan: Last Poems. Trans. Katherine Washburn and Margret Guillemin. San Francisco: North Point Press, 1986.

Friedrich Hölderlin

Sämtliche Werke. "Grosse Stuttgarter Ausgabe." Ed. Friedrich Beissner, followed by Adolph Beck. 15 vols. Stuttgart: Kohlhammer, 1946–57.

Sämtliche Werke. "Frankfurter historisch-kritische Ausgabe." Ed. D. E. Sattler and W. Greddeck. 20 vols. Frankfurt: Roter Stern, 1975.

Friedrich Hölderlin: Poems and Fragments. Trans. Michael Hamburger. Cambridge: Cambridge University Press, 1980.

Hölderlin: Hymns and Fragments. Trans. Richard Sieburth. Princeton: Princeton University Press, 1984.

Hölderlin: Essays and Letters on Theory. Trans. and ed. Thomas Pfau. Albany: SUNY Press, 1988.

Rainer Maria Rilke

Sämtliche Werke. 6 vols. Ed. Ernst Zinn. Zurich: Insel Verlag, 1956.

Rilke: Duino Elegies and the Sonnets to Orpheus. Trans. A. Poulin, Jr. Boston: Houghton Mifflin Co., 1977.

Georg Trakl

Dichtungen und Briefe. 2 vols. Ed. Walther Killy and Hans Szklenar. Salzburg: Otto Müller Verlag, 1969.

Song of the West; Selected Poems of Georg Trakl. Trans. Robert Firmage. San Francisco: North Point Press, 1988.

MONOGRAPHS

Allemann, Beda. *Hölderlin und Heidegger*. Zurich: Atlantis, 1954.

———. *Zeit und Figur beim späten Rilke*. Pfullingen: Neske, 1961.

Bataille, Georges. *Visions of Excess; Selected Writings, 1927–1939*. Ed. Allan Stoekl, trans. A. Stoekl, C. R. Lovitt, and D. M. Leslie, Jr. Minneapolis: University of Minnesota Press, 1985.

Blanchot, Maurice. *L'espace littéraire*. Paris: Gallimard, 1978.

———. *The Unavowable Community*. Trans. Pierre Joris. Barrytown, N. Y.: Station Hill Press, 1988.

———. *The Writing of the Disaster*. Trans. Ann Smock. Lincoln: University of Nebraska Press, 1986.

Baumann, Gerhardt. *Erinnerungen an Paul Celan*. Frankfurt a. M.: Suhrkamp, 1986.

Beaufret, Jean. *Dialogue avec Heidegger*. 3 vols. Paris: Minuit, 1973–74.

Bernasconi, Robert. *The Question of Language in Heidegger's History of Being*. Atlantic Highlands, N. J.: Humanities Press, 1985.

Bollack, Jean, and Heinz Wismann. *Héraclite ou la séparation*. Paris: Minuit, 1972.

Bruns, Gerald L. *Heidegger's Estrangements; Language, Truth, and Poetry in the Later Writings*. New Haven and London: Yale University Press, 1989.

Castoriades, Cornelius. *Crossroads in the Labyrinth*. Trans. Kate Soper and Martin H. Ryle. Cambridge, MA: MIT Press, 1984.

Dallmayr, Fred R. *Polis and Praxis; Exercises in Contemporary Political Theory*. Cambridge, MA: MIT Press, 1984.

De Man, Paul. *Allegories of Reading*. New Haven and London: Yale University Press, 1978.

———. *Blindness and Insight*. Minneapolis: University of Minnesota Press, 1971.

———. *Critical Writings, 1953–1978*. Ed. Lindsay Waters. Minneapolis: University of Minnesota Press, 1989.

————. *The Rhetoric of Romanticism*. New York: Columbia University Press, 1984.

Derrida, Jacques. *De l'esprit; Heidegger et la question*. Paris: Galilée, 1986.

————. *Margins of Philosophy*. Trans. Alan Bass. Chicago: University of Chicago Press, 1982.

————. *Shibboleth: pour Paul Celan*. Paris: Galilée, 1986.

————. *Writing and Difference*. Trans. Alan Bass. Chicago: University of Chicago Press, 1978.

Faden, Gerhard. *Der Schein der Kunst: zu Heideggers Kritik der Aesthetik*. Wurzburg: Königshausen und Neumann, 1986.

Farias, Victor. *Heidegger et le nazisme*. Paris: Verdier, 1987.

Fynsk, Christopher. *Heidegger: Thought and Historicity*. Ithaca: Cornell University Press, 1986.

Gadamer, Hans-Georg. *Kleine Schriften*. 4 vols. Tübingen: Mohr, 1967–71.

————. *Philosophical Hermeneutics*. Trans. and ed. by David E. Linge. Berkeley: University of California Press, 1976.

————. *Poetica. Ausgewählte Essays*. Zurich: Insel Verlag, 1977.

————. *The Relevance of the Beautiful, and Other Essays*. Ed. Robert Bernasconi, trans. Nicholas Walker. Cambridge: Cambridge University Press, 1986.

————. *Wer bin Ich und wer bist Du? Kommentar zu Celans "Atemkristall."* Frankfurt a. M.: Suhrkamp, 1973.

Gallop, David. *Parmenides of Elea. Fragments*. Toronto: University of Toronto Press, 1984.

Halliburton, David. *Poetic Thinking: An Approach to Heidegger*. Chicago: University of Chicago Press, 1981.

Hegel, Georg Wilhelm Friedrich. *Vorlesungen über die Aesthetik. Sämtliche Werke.* "Jubiläumsausgabe." Ed. Hermann Glockner. 4th ed. Stuttgart/Bad Canstatt: Friedrich Fromann Verlag, 1964. Vols. 12, 13.

Jabès, Edmond. *From the Desert to the Book; Dialogues with Marcel Cohen*. Trans. Pierre Joris. Barrytown, N. Y.: Station Hill Press, 1990.

Janicaud, Dominique, and J. F. Mattéi. *La métaphysique à la limite*. Paris: PUF, 1983.

Lacoue-Labarthe, Philippe. *Heidegger, Art and Politics*. Trans. Chris Turner. Oxford: Blackwell, 1990.

————. *La poésie comme expérience*. Paris: Bourgeois, 1986.

————. *L'imitation des modernes. Typographies II*. Paris: Galilée, 1986.

Levinas, Emmanuel. *Ethics and Infinity; Conversations with Richard Nemo*. Trans. Richard A. Cohen. Pittsburgh: Duquesne University Press, 1985.

———. *Otherwise than Being and Beyond Essence*. Trans. Alphonso Lingis. The Hague: Nijhoff, 1981.

———. *Time and the Other*. Trans. Richard A. Cohen. Pittsburgh: Duquesne University Press, 1987.

Löwith, Karl. *Mein Leben in Deutschland vor und nach 1933*. Stuttgart: Metzler, 1986.

Lyotard, Jean-François. *Heidegger et "les juifs."* Paris: Galilée, 1988.

Merleau-Ponty, Maurice. *The Visible and the Invisible*. Trans. Alphonso Lingis. Evanston: Northwestern University Press, 1986.

Palmier, Jean-Michel. *Les écrits politiques de Martin Heidegger*. Paris: Editions de l'Herne, 1968.

———. *Situation de Georg Trakl*. Paris: Editions de l'Herne, 1972.

Pöggeler, Otto. *Philosophie und Politik bein Heidegger*. Freiburg/Munich: Karl Alber, 1972.

———. *Spur des Worts; zur Lyrik Paul Celans*. Freiburg/Munich: Karl Alber, 1986.

Schier, Rudolf Dirk. *Die Sprache Georg Trakls*. Heidelberg: C. Winter, 1970.

Schmidt, Jochen. *Hölderlins letzte Hymnen*. Tübingen: Niemeyer, 1970.

Schürmann, Reiner. *Heidegger on Being and Acting; From Principles to Anarchy*. Trans. Christine-Marie Gros. Bloomington: Indiana University Press, 1987.

Szondi, Peter. *Celan-Studien*. Frankfurt a. M.: Suhrkamp, 1972.

———. *On Textual Understanding*. Translated by Harvey Mendelsohn. Minneapolis: University of Minnesota Press, 1986.

Warminski, Andrzej. *Readings in Interpretation: Hölderlin, Hegel, Heidegger*. Intro. Rodolphe Gasché. Minneapolis: University of Minnesota Press, 1987.

Wyschogrod, Edith. *Spirit in Ashes: Hegel, Heidegger, and Man-Made Mass Death*. New Haven and London: Yale University Press, 1985.

Zimmermann, Michael E. *Heidegger's Confrontation with Modernity: Technology, Politics, Art*. Bloomington: Indiana University Press, 1990.

EDITED COLLECTIONS

Böschenstein, Bernhard, and Jacques Le Rider, eds. *Hölderlin vu de France*. Tübingen: Günter Narr, 1987.

Brooks, P., S. Felman, and J. H. Miller, eds. *The Lesson of Paul de Man. Yale French Studies* 69 (1985).

Cascardi, Anthony J., ed. *Philosophy and the Question of Literature*. Baltimore: Johns Hopkins, 1987.

Colin, Amy D., ed. *Argumentum e Silentio; International Paul Celan Symposium*. Berlin: De Gruyter, 1987.

Courtine, Jean-François, ed. *L'Herne: Hölderlin*. Paris Editions de l'Herne, 1989.

Davidson, Arnold I., ed. "Symposium on Heidegger and Nazism." *Critical Inquiry* 13:2 (Winter 1989): 407–488.

"Dossier: Martin Heidegger." *Magazine Littéraire* 235 (November 1986): 16–56.

Füllborn, U., and M. Engel, eds. *Materialien zu Rainer Marie Rilkes "Duineser Elegien."* Frankfurt a. M.: Suhrkamp, 1980.

Gethmann-Siefert, Annemarie, ed. *Philosophie und Poesie; Otto Pöggeler zum 60. Geburtstag*; "Spekulation und Erfahrung," vols. 7, 8. Stuttgart-Bad Cannstatt: Fromann-Holzboog, 1988.

Gethmann-Siefert, Annemarie, and Otto Pöggeler, eds. *Heidegger und die praktische Philosophie*. Frankfurt a. M.: Suhrkamp, 1988.

Gorner, Rüdiger, ed. *Rainer Maria Rilke*. Darmstadt: Wissenschaftliche Buchgesellschaft, 1987.

Haar, Michel, ed. *L'Herne: Martin Heidegger*. Paris: Editions de l'Herne, 1983.

Hamacher, Werner, and Winfried Menninghaus, eds. *Paul Celan*. Frankfurt a. M.: Suhrkamp, 1988.

Jamme, Christoph, and Otto Pöggeler, eds. *Jenseits des Idealismus. Hölderlins letzte Homburger Jahre (1804–1806)*. Bonn: Bouvier, 1982.

"Heidegger: la philosophie et le nazisme." *Le Débat* 48 (January–February 1988): 112–192.

Klostermann, Vittorio, ed. *Durchblicke; Martin Heidegger zum 80. Geburtstag*. Frankfurt a. M.: Klostermann, 1970.

Merrill, Robert, ed. *Ethics/Aesthetics: Post-Modern Positions*. Washington, D. C.: Maisonneuve Press, 1988.

Murray, Michael, ed. *Heidegger and Modern Philosophy*. New Haven and London: Yale University Press, 1978.

Nancy, Jean-Luc, ed. "Topos: Who Comes After the Subject?" *Topoi*, 7:2 (September 1988).

Parkes, Graham, ed. *Heidegger and Asian Thought*. Honolulu: University of Hawaii Press, 1987.

Sallis, John, ed. "Heidegger and Hölderlin." *Research in Phenomenology* 19 (1989).

Sallis, John, and Kenneth Maly, eds. *Heraclitean Fragments; A Companion Volume to the Heidegger/Fink Seminar on Heraclitus*. University, Alabama: The University of Alabama Press, 1980.

Sheehan, Thomas, ed. *Heidegger: the Man and the Thinker*. Chicago: Precedent Publishing, Inc., 1981.

Spanos, William, ed. *Martin Heidegger and the Question of Literature*. Bloomington: Indiana University Press, 1986.

Speier, Hans-Michael, ed. *Celan-Jahrbuch 1; Celan-Jahrbuch 2.* Heidelberg: Karl Winter Universitatsverlag, 1987, 1988.

Strelka, Joseph, P., ed. *Internationales Trakl-Symposium.* "Internationales Jahrbuch fur Germanistik," A XII. Berne: Peter Lang, 1984.

Weis, Walter, and Hans Weichselbaum, Hans, eds. *Salzburger Trakl-Symposion.* Salzburg: Otto Müller, 1978.

Wolin, Richard, ed. "The French Heidegger Debate." *New German Critique* 45 (Fall 1988): 135–161.

———. "Martin Heidegger and Politics: A Dossier." *New German Critique* 55 (Fall 1988): 91–161.

ARTICLES

Articles that appear in the edited collections cited above are not listed here. Cited articles in edited collections are referenced and discussed in the Notes, above.

Biemel, Walter. "Zu Heideggers Deutung der Ister-Hymne." *Heidegger Studies* 3/4 (1987/88): 41–57.

Derrida, Jacques. "The Politics of Friendship." *The Journal of Philosophy* 85:11 (November 1988): 638–649.

Fóti, Véronique M. "Alètheia and Oblivion's Field: On Heidegger's Parmenides Lectures." *Ethics and Danger,* 1989 SPEP Series volume, forthcoming, 1991.

———. "Politics at the Limits of Metaphysics: Heidegger, Ferry & Renaut, and Lyotard." *The Graduate Faculty Philosophy Journal* 14:2–15:1 (1991): 323–334.

———. "Representation and the Image: Between Heidegger, Derrida, and Plato." *Man and World* 18 (1985): 65–78.

———. "The Path of the Stranger: On Heidegger's Interpretation of Georg Trakl." *Review of Existential Psychology and Psychiatry* 17:2/3 (1983): 223–233.

Harries, Karsten. "Heidegger as a Political Thinker." *Review of Metaphysics* 30:4 (June 1976): 642–669.

Ott, Hugo. "Martin Heidegger als Rektor der Universität Freiburg." *Zeitschrift für Geschichte des Oberrheins* 132 (1984): 95–128.

———. "Martin Heidegger und die Universität Freiburg nach 1945." *Historisches Jahrbuch* 105 (1985): 95–128.

Pöggeler, Otto. "Heidegger's Begegnung mit Hölderlin." *Man and World* 10 (1977): 13–61.

———. "Den Führer führen? Heidegger und kein Ende." *Philosophische Rundschau* 32 (1985): 26–67.

———. "Neue Wege mit Heidegger?" *Philosophische Rundschau* 29 (1982): 39–71.

Schmidt, Jochen. "Der Begriff des Zorns in Hölderlins Spätwerk." *Hölderlin-Jahrbuch* 15 (1967–68): 128–157.

Schürmann, Reiner. "Riveted to a Monstrous Site: On Heidegger's *Beiträge zur Philosophie*." Paper presented at a conference on Heidegger and practical life; Greater Philadelphia Philosophy Consortium, 18 March 1989.

———. "Situating René Char: Hölderlin, Heidegger, Char, and the 'There Is'." *Boundary 2* 4:2 (Winter 1976): 513–534.

Sheehan, Thomas. "Heidegger and the Nazis." *New York Review of Books* (June 1988): 38–44.

Wright, Kathleen. "Reading Heidegger Reading Hölderlin." *Art, Politics, Technology: Martin Heidegger, 1889–1989*. Ed. Karsten Harries and Otto Pöggeler. Forthcoming.

———. "The Place of the Work of Art in the Age of Technology." *Southern Journal of Philosophy* 22 (Winter 1984): 563–583.

Zimmermann, Michael E. "Heidegger, Ethics, and National Socialism." *Southern Journal of Philosophy* 5 (Spring 1976): 97–106.

Index of Persons

◆

Index of Topics

◆